HouseBeautiful
Decorating School

House Beautiful
Decorating School

Tessa Evelegh

HEARST BOOKS
A division of Sterling Publishing Co., Inc.

New York / London
www.sterlingpublishing.com

Created, edited, and designed by
Duncan Baird Publishers Ltd., Castle House, 75-76 Wells Street,
London W1T 3QH

Managing Editor: Emma Callery
Designer: Alison Shackleton
Illustrations: Kate Simunek

Photographs: See credits on page 247. The publisher has made
every effort to properly credit the photographers whose work appears
in this book. Please let us know if an error has been made, and we
will make any necessary changes in subsequent printings.

Library of Congress has catalogued the hardcover edition as follows:
Evelegh, Tessa.
House beautiful decorating school / Tessa Evelegh.
p. cm.
Includes index.
ISBN 1-58816-360-1
1. Interior decoration—United States—History—20th century. I.
Title: Decorating school. II. Hearst Books (Firm) III. House beautiful.
IV. Title
NK2004.E94 2004
747—dc22

2004004114

10 9 8 7 6 5 4 3 2 1

First Paperback Edition 2008
Published by Hearst Books
A Division of Sterling Publishing Co., Inc.
387 Park Avenue South, New York, NY 10016

House Beautiful and Hearst Books
are trademarks of Hearst Communications, Inc.

www.housebeautiful.com

For information about custom editions, special sales, premium
and corporate purchases, please contact Sterling Special Sales
Department at 800-805-5489 or specialsales@sterlingpub.com.

Distributed in Canada by Sterling Publishing
c/o Canadian Manda Group, 165 Dufferin Street
Toronto, Ontario, Canada M6K 3H6

Distributed in Australia by Capricorn Link (Australia) Pty. Ltd.
P.O. Box 704, Windsor, NSW 2756 Australia

Manufactured in China

Sterling ISBN 13: 978-1-58816-511-4
ISBN 10: 1-58816-511-6

Contents

Foreword

Welcome to Decorating School—*the book that gives you the how, what, where, and when of interior design.*

The idea of getting the house, or even one room, redecorated is always exciting. Out with the old, the tired-around-the-edges, the finger-marked, the grubby, or the chipped; and in with the fresh, the new, the clean, the latest colors, the inspired solutions. This is our vision and this is what inspires us to take on a decorating project. But anyone who's ever tackled decorating has to admit that between the thrill of thinking through exciting new changes and being able to sit back and relax in a lovely new home, there is usually a low point. Even when only one room is being tackled, there's a domino effect that seems to permeate the whole house; the job always seems to take longer, cost more, and involve at least one heated discussion with the contractors.

But it doesn't have to be that way. *Decorating School* is about turning your dreams into reality. It is a step-by-step guide that takes you from formulating your vision and developing your own personal style to outlining the priorities when considering each room. It is also a useful reference book that includes a guide to the wide choice of generic products available, so you can visit suppliers armed with an understanding of the kind of look that suits your style and how to attain it. Finally, *Decorating School* helps you to think through what professional help you may need, find the right people, brief them properly, and manage the budgets for a smoothly running job.

Redecorating has a spring cleaning effect—it's a time when we can completely rethink our lifestyle. This may be simply because we've emptied the room, overcome our storage problems, and come up with better solutions, which can be built into the decorating project. Or it may be a turning point in our lives: the children, for example, may need a very different bedroom as they move on to high school. Redecoration of the home office may also be the time to plan for accommodating new technology, possibly streamlining the burden of household accounts and management.

These are the issues that *Decorating School* addresses. It's about helping you to think through what you need right now and how to use the space in your home most effectively for the benefit of the whole family. It's about finding a style that suits your life today in a practical way, which is so much more than simply pragmatic.

The Editors of *House Beautiful*

The Art of
the Possible

Perfect Home Basics

Decorating is a wonderfully refreshing experience. Despite all the mess and disruption, when it's finished everything looks so much better, is more organized, and says something both about how we feel and how we are now—not how we were when we last decorated. And that is the key. Before you begin, spend as much time as you can researching how you want your home to look, bearing in mind that you are unlikely to redecorate again for several years. Also, perhaps even more importantly, some of the furnishing purchases you make now may be with you for a considerable time, if not for the rest of your life. So look through books, magazines, in shops, and other homes, and try to analyze what really suits you and your lifestyle.

Do you want your home to look sophisticated above anything else, or do you prefer a more relaxed feel? Do you love minimalism, with everything stacked neatly behind cupboard doors, or are you a bit of a squirrel—a clutter queen who likes to enjoy lovingly collected memorabilia? Do you like open spaces, or cozy corners? Are you wedded to your favorites, or do you prefer all that is new? Do you find strong color invigorating, or are you more relaxed in neutral environments? The answer to all these questions will help point you in the general direction of your own style.

▲ On display
Even the most functional possessions can look lovely. Here, white plates and glasses, stainless steel mixing bowls, and vases are stacked onto open shelves to make an appealing display. From a practical point of view, everything is near at hand, easy to find, and easy to put away.

◀ Sleek simplicity
Plenty of flush-fronted kitchen closets offer quick-fix tidying for a sleek, modern look that's easy to keep up.

▶ New England classics
Elegant, classic New England style is rooted in the eighteenth-century European Georgian period, and so includes antique or reproduction furniture. The purchase of this style of furniture is a big investment, so the best plan is to research what you really like before setting off for auctions, antique fairs, or antique shops.

When it comes to the actual purchases, take your time if you want to avoid making mistakes. Again, research is everything. Magazines are a great source for finding retail outlets that suit your style. Go and visit as many as you can, but don't take your checkbook with you—it's all too easy to be persuaded into making a hasty purchase. Look at each item from every angle, to see that it is beautiful whichever way you look at it. Take note of how it will look from where you would normally see it. Dining chairs, for example, are often displayed on high shelves, so you'll be viewing them from quite the wrong angle. Set them on the floor before making a decision. Carpets should be put on the floor, and fabrics viewed from a distance of at least six feet.

Take a digital camera if you can, and make a file of your favorites, slowly making up a storyboard of a look you like. If you're not excited about anything you see, make do with what you have until you find what you really want. You may have to wait months, but it is only when you're absolutely sure you adore a piece that you should buy it.

▼ **Simple comfort**

Make the most of the space in a small bedroom by hanging a huge mirror to give the impression of added space and light. The bed provides the focal point, and all the clutter is put away neatly in generous closets fitted along the full length of the wall opposite the bed.

▲ Color story

Green kitchen cabinets mark out the working area of a larger, open-plan living room kitchen. The whole space is painted buttermilk yellow for continuity: the brighter kitchen area adds vigor to the working part of the living space.

◄ Easy living

The relaxed look is made up of tidy surfaces accessorized by just one or two beautiful possessions. It is not nearly as demanding as modern minimalism, nor as busy as the cluttered look.

Thinking Big

Redecorating not only changes the way you feel about your home, it can also have an effect on your lifestyle, so this is a time to think big. Whether you're planning a new kitchen, office, or playroom, or you are going for a complete remodel of the whole house, you're more likely to get the best results by thinking through your lifestyle. Consider both the way it is now and how you might like it to be in five years' time. This is relevant for all age groups. If you have children, the play areas in their rooms may need to become workstations before five years are out. So, plan in plenty of desk space that can be used for drawing and crafts now, and homework in a few years. Shelf space that is home to cuddly toys today can be laden with books tomorrow. If you're past that stage, and nearer retirement, you may want to trade sleeping space for living space as you'll be spending more time at home. Or you may require more office space as all that domestic paperwork expands.

In addition to these practical considerations, your lifestyle may also have a bearing on how you want the room to look once you have decorated it. Your style may have changed recently for many reasons. As well as being affected by changes in interior fashion, you may also have practical reasons for reviewing your style. If you are a family with children, the clutter you loved before they came along may just drive you crazy now that there's lots of toy tidying. Or the children may have grown up enough for you to be able to put your favorite things back on display without fear of mishaps.

▶ **Flexible living**

This loft-style apartment was bought as a shell to offer a lifetime of flexibility. A single wall incorporating plenty of closet space was the only permanent fixture. The space can be divided using screens such as this shelving unit and adapted to the owner's needs as they change over the years.

▶▶ **Bold start**

A huge space such as this is a luxury indeed, but it would be all too easy to fill it up with clutter. A few beautiful pieces of furniture, perfectly positioned, are all that is needed for single-space living. The kitchen provides the core, with the dining area on one side, the living area on the other. The whole apartment has been unified with simple white walls and black furniture.

◀ Eclectic character

Open-plan living does not have to be all modern and minimalist. This room is furnished with traditional furniture, yet offers the flexibility of a modern lifestyle. Kitchen, dining, and seating areas have been arranged within a single space so that the different elements can be enlarged or reduced to suit the occasion.

▼ Restful changes

Where copious seating is demanded, arrange it in small groups, giving each its own character by using different colors or styles. Otherwise, the roomscape could become monotonous.

Do you like the kitchen as it is, or would you prefer to introduce new elements, such as dining or seating areas, to accommodate your current lifestyle? Does your office provide enough space for all the latest office machinery, and, if not, do you want the new storage to show it or hide it? Do you really want the laundry area in the basement when all the clothes and linens are stored at the top of the house? These might not seem like decorating decisions, but they can make a big difference as to how you decide to tackle any new plans you may have for your home.

Whatever you decide to do, write down what you like about how each room is organized now and what is irritating to you. Find out about how the rest of the household would like to use the rooms in question, and aim to incorporate the changes when you come to decorate. Even if that means you have to beg, borrow, or save extra money to achieve all your aims, it could be cheaper in the long run. If you don't face up to the decisions now, you could risk papering over the problems, only to find you need to redecorate sooner, rather than later.

Working with Space

It is true that we all need a certain minimum amount of space, but clever designers seem to be able to conjure extra space out of nowhere and, with lateral thinking, so can we. It all comes back again to thinking about what you would ideally like from your home. Where do you need more space and where could you afford to let a little go? Do you have, for example, roomy landings that can be fitted with wall-to-wall cupboards and put to all kinds of uses, such as linen cupboards, overflow clothes closets, or bedding storage? You may even be able to squeeze small rooms out of landing or under-stair space for laundry areas, home offices, filing systems, toilets, or even shower rooms. Hidden behind flush doors that are painted to match the rest of the area, you'll hardly miss the space, but it could relieve congestion elsewhere in the house. Apply the same idea in any place where there may be stealable space—at the end of a roomy kitchen, for example.

Alternatively, use space by going the other way and opening up your surroundings. If two small rooms no longer suit your lifestyle, consider hiring builders to knock down the wall between them and create one large space. If getting the builders in is rather more ambitious than your decorating plans allow, make efficient use of space on a much smaller scale. Divide rooms and spaces using screens, sliding doors, or fabric panels hung from the ceiling. Steal alcoves, nooks, and crannies for storage, filling them with books, china, and glass. In this way you free up cupboard space elsewhere in the house.

▼◄ **Wall space**

This tiny attic room barely has space for two beds, and certainly not enough for bedside tables. The solution? Bedside lamps are wall-mounted above the headboards to dispense with the need for the tables.

▼ **Partitioned off**

Where space is tight, partition it with translucent materials for a feeling of light. Here, pink glass adds emphasis to a shower cubicle.

► **Sliding doors**

Sliding doors make for the most versatile space of all, as rooms can be changed from one to two within seconds. Most of the time, this one is left open to create a large, open space, but it is closed to create privacy when dining.

Space-hungry children's rooms can be made to work very hard, thereby doubling the useable areas. Loft beds allow for desks, closets, spare beds, or even sofa beds underneath, freeing floor space for play. If the headroom will not accommodate the height of a loft bed, look for cabin beds instead, which come ready-stacked on chests of drawers, making good use of vertical space. Desks can easily be built in to make excellent use of "dead" walls or corners. Buy trestle or table legs and screw them to wooden or medium-density fiberboard tops—which can then be painted or stained to match the room's color scheme—and the children will have ample room for craft work, homework, and computers once they're old enough.

Some living rooms can be reorganized to proffer more space, too. If the current arrangement is not working, consider different furniture. Would two sofas serve your space better than the ubiquitous three-piece suite, or would your seating area work even more efficiently with a corner or sectional sofa? Where space is really tight, think vertically and fit floor-to-ceiling shelves, sectioned off so you can stack and store away your possessions. If too much space is your problem, look at creating a more cozy seating area with the judicious placing of shelving units that double as room dividers. For that party you are planning, they can be pushed back out of the way.

◀ Spaced out

Sometimes, the best use of space is to keep it as empty as possible. The only furniture that is needed for this extension is a dining table and chairs for relaxed dining.

▼◀ Shape works

Make a virtue of oddly shaped rooms. This L-shape divides naturally into a seating and a dining area, offering the potential for individual furnishing styles.

▼ Moving walls

Painted to match the rest of the room, this sliding wall looks just like all the rest when the kitchen is closed off from the dining area. It is a sophisticated and deceptively simple solution.

21

Working with Scale

Sensitivity to scale and efficient use of space go hand in hand when it comes to planning successful interiors. Fittings and furniture that are chosen and designed to suit the scale of the room not only look better, but also make the best use of space. Bulky furniture in cottage-sized rooms will never allow for enough seating, whereas furniture designed to have more dainty proportions might even provide surplus seating, useful for when guests come to call. At the other end of the scale, small furniture in a large room will look lost, resulting in a choppy overall look.

When buying new furniture, therefore, keep scale in mind. But you must also ensure that it works well with what you already have. Perfectly matching furniture isn't necessarily a better option than mismatched, and, if you're buying over the years, often not possible. But if you keep scale and proportion in mind, the results can be remarkably harmonious. Balance is the key.

It's not just the size of furniture you need to consider; it's also the bulk. If your furniture tends to have strong, bold proportions, don't be tempted to add finer pieces.

▲ Perfect fit
A tiny alcove can be turned into a useful dining area if furniture is bought to suit the space. This simple, curvy table and set of colorful chairs perfectly fit the bill.

◀ Small beauty
This narrow room provides plenty of seating space, yet its proportions are far from generous. The secret of its success has been to furnish it just with a small oval table and several delicate dining chairs. A narrow console can be used for serving.

▶ Great combination
When lots of small elements add up to a slightly incongruous whole, use scale to pull the look together. Here, two paintings look almost outsized on a narrow pillar, but they provide impact where it's needed.

Bear in mind that exposed legs on an upholstered chair or sofa will generally make it look lighter and less dominating than pieces that have skirts instead.

If you are planning to furnish any room from scratch, make sure that you allow for plenty of circulation and "useable" space between furniture and fixtures. There's no point, for example, in planning a kitchen island unit if that means everything has to be so close together that oven and dishwasher doors can't open properly. This might sound obvious, but even the most careful builders have been known to forget to check some of these most essential details. Even if the doors do open and the island unit gives you ample work space, the surrounding area may then look cramped and be almost impossible to move around in. It's much better, where proportions are tight, to select a simpler solution, such as a galley kitchen.

Accessories are the one element where it is possible to break the proportion rules. While accessories that are in proportion with the size of the room and furniture tend to look the best, this does not always have to be the case. Hanging one huge painting or mirror in a small room, for example, has a clutter-free look that perversely lends a sense of openness and grandeur. You can also use small items in generous spaces, although, if you want them to create impact, group such miscellanea by arranging them in a cabinet or on shelves to give the illusion of one large item. Collections of small prints can also look good in large rooms if they are seen as one big item, so to give maximum impact, mount them in matching frames.

25

◀ Giant moves

Here, a huge fireplace dwarfs the seating, adding to the impact of a striking, modern living room. The only ornaments are also outsized: a large, oval wall plaque, and big vases on the coffee table.

▶ Outsized accessories

The restrained décor of this dining room means that the large photograph, light fixture, and table centerpiece make the maximum impact: scale at its best.

Show It or Hide It

A fundamental decision you need to make before embarking on any kind of interior decorating is whether you like clean minimalism or a cozier, more cluttered look. This may have as much to do with your lifestyle and stage of life as your own sense of style. Do you like to have everything on view and at hand, or do you prefer to have it neatly stacked behind cupboard doors for quick-fix tidying and cleaning?

When you are considering your options, bear in mind that the clean, minimalist look might, on the face of it, appear to make tidying easier, but it is very unforgiving of anything left lying around. Absolutely everything really does have to be swept away for it to look its best. A little bit of clutter, on the other hand, is always happy to be joined by a little more.

▶ **All on display**
Even if you're not a trinket lover, you may enjoy the look of practical household items. Stacked onto compartmentalized shelving, they can make a striking display.

▼ **Behind closed doors**
This range of cupboards and worktop-cum-breakfast-bar have the effect of a huge, well-proportioned sculpture.

If you're a hide-it person, you need to consider storage and closets before you even begin to think about decorating. Discreet wall-to-wall cupboards are essential for the minimalist lifestyle, and can even improve the proportions of the room. A long, thin room, for example, can be immeasurably improved by fitting a wall of cupboards all along one of the short walls. In space-hungry bathrooms, fitted cupboards disguised as walls or even mirrors give ample room for the less-than-beautiful washing paraphernalia to be stashed away.

If you're a show-it type, you may want to build in plenty of shelves so that everything can be shown off or displayed. This might be the best solution if you love all the practical elements of life. Casseroles and vases, plates and bowls can be very decorative. Stacked onto shelves designed to suit their proportions, they can add interest to a room, especially if they are linked in some way, such as by color or style. Group them into types: for example, you may like to keep all your vases together, or line up a row of pretty jugs. Alternatively, you could group them by material, putting all your glass on one shelf, white china on another, and colored china on a third.

▼ Showing off
A table behind the sofa is set with an interesting ensemble of objects, providing a delightful montage that makes a friendly welcome into the room. Artifacts add personality to a room, speaking volumes about their owner.

▲ Calmer clutter

If you love to have your things all around you, but sometimes find the clutter distracting, think color coordination. Here, by displaying only cream-colored items on the shelves, a disparate collection of books and objets d'art take on a far more cohesive look.

◀ Prized possessions

Lovingly collected artifacts deserve to be displayed, so incorporate them into the interior design. These shelves have been fixed at just the right heights for a collection of stone vases, creating a striking display.

Style & Mood

The Art of Color

For quick-fix style change, there's little more immediately impressive than a fresh coat of paint. Moving into a new home or room, most of us come armed with color charts, paints, and brushes, as this is the best way to quickly make it ours. But choosing colors can be a tricky business. The human eye can differentiate among thousands of shades, and all too often, a color choice can just "miss." Here are some ideas for achieving a successful color scheme.

■ Gather inspiration by looking through books and magazines and noting what color combinations you like in other homes, shops, cafés, and restaurants.

■ Decide what kinds of colors you like. Do you prefer lights and brights, or warmer and cozier colors? If you've always loved blue, don't let its reputation for being cool put you off. Even chilly, north-facing rooms can look good in blue if you choose the warmer tones, such as lavender, or compensate with warm accents, such as raspberry.

■ If you lack color confidence, choose a scheme made up of just one color. Introduce interest by using various tones of that same color and either white for a fresh scheme, or black for a moodier look.

▲ Bright with white

If you love bright color, but feel overwhelmed when completely surrounded by it, simply add a strong tone to a mainly white interior. The white intensifies the color, making a dramatic statement that's nevertheless easy to live with.

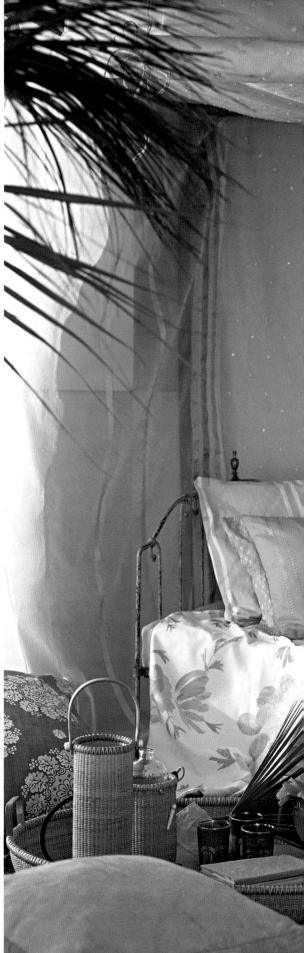

▲ Harmonious pastels

Pastel pink, purple, and aqua add up to a pretty, relaxing scheme because they are close in tone. The white freshens up the overall look.

◄ Accent

Accents bring sparkle to color schemes. Here, sharp lime green adds zest to a pretty aquamarine room, intensifying the turquoise tones. The finished effect is one of harmony, achieved by choosing colors of a similar intensity.

■ Schemes of many colors are more relaxing to live with if they are all kept to a similar tone—for example, several different pastels look good together as will several different brights, but mixing them demands confidence.

■ Contrast creates impact. Either use light and dark shades of similar colors, or go for contrasting colors, such as black and white, red and green, or yellow and purple.

■ Upholstery and curtain fabrics can be useful starting points for an interesting scheme, as you can match paint colors to the different elements of the design.

■ Colors can take on a variety of personalities, so test how they will look in a room by painting part of the wall and looking at it over the course of twenty-four hours. Note how the color looks during various times of the day, as natural light falls into the room, and take a look at it again in the evening, when the lights are turned on.

◀ Contrasting impact

White contrasts with a charcoal-and-burnt-orange color combination, setting off a confident scheme. It works because the orange provides a bright, modern element.

▲ Bright new looks

Bright pink, green, yellow, and purple are similar in tone, so they sit happily together in the same room. The gray walls create a witty backdrop to the multicolored foreground.

Contrasting Texture

Texture introduces a tactile dimension to interiors, bringing a sensual element to a room. Sumptuous velvet cushions are irresistible to the touch, and, lying next to smooth, shiny silk, they can add visual drama. Texture always works well when it is used in contrast: set shiny leather furniture against a deep-pile carpet or rug, or chunky-weave upholstery fabrics against smooth, shiny paint. This contrast adds to the play of light and shade within the room, and is particularly effective in paler color schemes, such as creams, whites, and neutrals.

■ Even a shiny mirror brings contrast to a subtle matte interior.

■ Textures don't have to make a huge statement. Just as accent colors add "seasoning" to the main color schemes, so pinpricks of texture can enrich an interior. Look for accessories with texture, such as shiny metal picture frames or interesting glass bead trims stitched to simple woven fabrics.

■ There are fashions in texture, just as there are in pattern and color. If you want to update a room, just add some of the latest textures in the form of a throw, rug, or accessory. This is far more subtle, and therefore less likely to become outmoded, than color or pattern.

◀ Color and texture

The texture of this coarse-weave carpet is accentuated by the use of contrasting yarns, creating a checkerboard effect.

◀◀ Smooth and shiny

Floor-to-ceiling shiny glass and metallic uprights are contrasted by a richly textured rug, turning what could be a sterile environment into one that is far more cozy and inviting.

▲ Hard choice

Texture doesn't have to be soft. Stone, pebbles, and shells are hard materials that can be used to create interesting effects. Here, pebbles have been used to decorate the walls in a washroom.

Perfect Patterns

The selective use of pattern brings flair to an interior. It breaks up solid color and so, perversely, allows you to use stronger shades. Whether you use classic weaves (such as tickings or ginghams), timeless ethnic prints (such as ikats or batiks), bold modern geometric patterns, or pretty country prints is really a matter of personal taste, but how you use them can make or break the overall look of the interior. Here are some guidelines.

■ Generally, it's a good idea to fit the scale of the pattern to the size of the room. Large patterns are likely to overwhelm small rooms, while small-scale patterns can be lost when viewed from a distance in a large room.

■ This "rule" can be broken if you have the confidence to make a loud design statement. A huge motif can look very good in a modern minimal interior or in a generously proportioned room with high ceilings.

■ Too many different florals in one room can look a little confusing. However, it is easy to successfully combine florals with geometrics. Choose stripes to make them sleek, and ginghams or even polka dots for a country look.

▶ China blue

China blue and white is such an enduring color partnership that it can be found in patterns from all around the world. This delightful color combination provides a link so patterns can be happily mixed.

▼ Bold move

Geometric patterns are always bold: use them in contrasting black and white and you're sure to make a statement. For a striking dining area within the kitchen, this checkerboard tabletop has been complemented by seat cushions in a colorful harlequin design.

■ When combining two or more patterns, help them to stand out from each other by varying the scale. When paired with a large motif, fine, allover designs take on a textural appearance.

■ Another way to link patterns is to combine several different designs in the same color.

■ Geometric patterns, such as checks and stripes, look great together. One pretty way of using them is, for example, to choose the same small-scale geometric design in two or three different pastels.

■ When buying patterned fabric, look at it in the way it will be seen in the room. For instance, if drapes are to be gathered, scrunch up a short length to see how the design might be distorted. Likewise, if you're planning to have Roman shades, fold the fabric to see how the design will look when they are drawn up.

▲ Mixed solution
Geometrics contrast well with busier patterns. Here, a floral cushion is crisply set off by the checked seat cover.

◄ Floral and geometric mix
The combination of florals and geometrics is a perennial favorite, as it is pretty without being overly fussy. Keep the look unified by having all the patterns in the same shade.

◄◄ Romance personified
Toile de Jouy is a classic pastoral design dating back to the early nineteenth century. It has a delicate, broken-up pattern, and can be used successfully on its own to soften a plain room—or on several different items, as here—without looking "overdone."

A Touch of Comfort

Above all else, home has to be the place where you can relax. It needs to express your design style without becoming a maintenance burden. While the days of the cluttered look are over, the rigors of minimalism can be too demanding for day-to-day life. Strike a balance by making sure there's plenty of cupboard space for all the unglamorous bits and pieces and adequate shelf space for sentimental treasures that turn your house into a home, and then choose easy-maintenance furnishings. Add plenty of items that invite relaxation, such as plush sofas, cushions, table lamps, and the latest magazines. Softness underfoot in the form of carpets and rugs just beg you to kick off your shoes for the ultimate in comfort.

▲ Relaxed dining

Fully upholstered chairs used for dining immediately suggest a long and lazy meal with family and friends. This fresh take on dining room seating—complete with matching cushions for extra back support while eating—is both inviting and comfortable.

▲ Bathroom living

The most comfortable bathrooms are those that have a touch of the living room about them. Full drapes, wallpaper, and homey touches all add up to that relaxed, lived-in feeling.

◀ Sumptuous sleeping

Something soft underfoot is always irresistible in the bedroom, and this rich, deep-pile rug is the ultimate in luxury. Offering barefoot pampering at the beginning and end of the day, it eases you into the morning and has a gloriously unwinding effect when the day is done.

Bedroom Comfort

REFERENCE POINT

■ If you need to install some bedroom storage, also read pages 212–213.

■ Bedroom lighting should be soft and romantic, but have task lighting in appropriate places. See Lighting on pages 146–153.

■ If you have a wooden floor, try to avoid having bare floorboards in the bedroom, as they can be drafty. More advice is on pages 82–83.

Comfort and a sense of calm are bedroom prerequisites. However, these essentials can be in conflict because clutter is the antithesis of calm, and yet clean minimalism can look anything but comfortable. The key is to provide plenty of storage to deal with the clutter. You can never have too many bedroom closets. As well as clothes and shoes, there are spare blankets or comforters to consider, jewelry, face creams, and even reading matter. If you're decorating from scratch, make the inclusion of capacious bedroom closets a priority. Clever designers can disguise closets by custom-fitting them and painting them to match the walls.

The more that can be secreted away, the better, leaving a clean canvas for bedroom essentials: the bed, bedside tables, and possibly a dressing table. An upholstered chair or sofa can also add to the comfort factor in an uncluttered way.

The next step is to develop a simple color scheme. Bright colors and too much pattern can be distracting, and certainly not conducive to sleep, so choose naturals, whites, pastels, or warm, earthy shades.

> Upholstered chairs or sofas add to the comfort factor in the bedroom.

Once the basic design and decorations have been selected, increase the bedroom comfort with plenty of inviting sink-back-and-relax comforters, pillows, and cushions. By using matching or color-coordinated pillows and cushions, you can pile on as many as you like and still avoid the cluttered look.

Provide interest with different-sized pillows—square, rectangular, and miniature—cased in coordinating fabrics and stacked one against the other. Pillows filled with natural feathers are generally softer than their synthetic cousins. If you prefer a firmer pillow to sleep on, you can still have visual interest by simply stacking sumptuous feather-filled ones on top of firmer synthetics.

Bedrooms need to be soft underfoot, too, for all those barefoot moments. If wooden floors are more your style than wall-to-wall carpets, choose some laminate flooring and then a large, deep-pile rug for the center of the room to sink your feet into as you get in and out of bed. This will help considerably on chilly winter mornings.

BEDROOM CARPETS AND RUGS

Since we spend much of our time in the bedroom barefoot, carpet is the most obvious choice. It is not as subject to heavy soiling or wear and tear as in other parts of the house, so it should keep its looks, even when it is not the highest quality (see page 86). Help it to remain looking good with regular vacuuming, which will help to reduce dirt, and by immediately mopping up spills with warm water. Any liquid allowed to soak into the fibers is likely to later attract dirt and grime.

Tufted Woven carpets with a cut pile. These include densely woven velvets and harder-wearing twists.

Looped Looped piles are uncut, giving a bouclé appearance. They provide a long-lasting, hardwearing finish.

Shag pile Soft, deep-pile carpets that became popular in the 1970s. Choose a dense weave, or they become flattened.

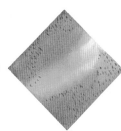

Chenille Soft, velvety, and often with a sheen, chenille carpets and rugs can be made from 100% cotton.

NOW LOOK AGAIN

Plenty of pillows look very inviting. By choosing several different sizes, you can increase the comfort without making the pile look untidy.

Comforters are aptly named, and you don't have to restrict yourself to just one per bed. A second one folded up at the end adds to the comfort zone.

Whether you have room for a large plush sofa or neat nursing chair, upholstered furniture always gives a sense of luxury.

A Touch of Drama

If exciting interiors are more your style than cozy ones, you'll need to inject a little drama. There are several ways to do this. You can choose striking color schemes, introducing plenty of contrast using reds, oranges, and bright yellows; or moody tones, such as deep plums, royal purples, or indigoes. Alternatively, opt for bold statements: such as a huge painting or a fabric with a large, extroverted motif. Another way to add drama is to veer toward the theatrical. A popular way to do this is to choose a theme to follow through. You could be inspired by baroque, ancient Roman, whimsical fairy-tale, or even a strong historical style, such as Art Deco, Art Nouveau, or high Victorian. Give your theme extra drama through the clever use of lighting: highlight focal points within the room.

◀ Color statement

Black and white form the ultimate contrast, and red is always a demanding color, so this combination is a brave one indeed. It works because the elements in the room are very simple and the red is limited to three distinct areas, which the eye can assimilate.

◀◀ Staged set

The ornate, painted mirror surround and voluptuous piles of fruit and flowers on the side table, set off by a pair of table lamps, gives a truly theatrical feeling to this particular room.

▲ Big motif

A large-scale motif, whether it be in the form of a painting, as here, or used on a fabric, always makes a statement. Here, it is further emphasized by the lively green and yellow color scheme on the walls, chair upholstery, and equally bold carpet.

Watery Paradise

REFERENCE POINT

■ Creating a mural of this size is tantamount to incorporating an architectural detail in your home. Read pages 102–103 for information about scale and style.

■ Prepare the wall before painting it. You might want to hang some lining paper and paint onto that rather than painting directly onto a plastered finish. Then it is time to choose your paints—see pages 94–95 for advice.

Any theme can be used for a dramatic look, and while we usually associate strong colors with drama, this does not always have to be the case. At home, where rooms are on a domestic scale, a little more subtlety is often called for, and murals in gentler tones can be just as effective as strident schemes. Watery tones of blue, green, and aqua are easy to live with, which makes this whimsical underwater theme a perfect choice for an informal dining room. You don't have to be an accomplished artist to create a simple mural like this particular one. Uncomplicated motifs like fish and corals are not difficult to produce freehand; but, with a little "cheating," it can be possible to reproduce even challenging images. One of the most popular ways is the use of stencils, many of which can be found in decorating and craft shops. However, this can limit your scheme to the stencil motifs you can find and to the sizes available. One solution would be to design and cut your own stencils, or, if you have access to an overhead projector (possibly borrowed from a college, church, or office), search for images from illustrated books and project the silhouettes onto the wall that you are decorating. Look for interesting motifs in volumes of antique prints, books, and magazines.

Children's books are also an excellent source of attractive illustrations, and are the perfect solution for decorating children's rooms, as their favorite characters can be included. Once the images are projected onto the wall, draw around the outlines in pencil, and then paint them at your leisure. Generally, the smaller the motif, the stronger the color you can use without it overpowering the overall scheme of the room.

Murals need to be planned around the architectural features within the room. All rooms have windows and doors that can be highlighted, but here the design has been used to accentuate the pretty porthole window at the top of the room. The blue-gray baroque-style framing of the window has been continued down the eaves to encompass the whole top section of the wall, creating a framework for the fish and coral.

> Murals in gentle tones can be just as effective as strident schemes.

HARD FLOORING

Original stone or ceramic flooring on the ground floors of old houses was very often taken from a local quarry. This gave the buildings a harmony with their geographical location. Take this as a lead when choosing hard floors, which are solid, resilient, long lasting, and likely to be in the house through many interior fashion changes. If it's no longer possible to get hold of local stone, select a hard floor that is compatible with the local building materials (see page 78).

Stone Very often comes from a local quarry, so the colors available may depend on where you live.

Ceramics These come in an infinite range of colors, from earth-toned designs to brightly colored mosaics.

Slate Very often charcoal-gray, though it can range from brown-gray through blue-gray to green-gray.

Quarry tiles Quarry tiles are made from unrefined, extruded alumina clay, creating a rich red-brown floor.

NOW LOOK AGAIN

Simple sea motifs are easy to re-create freehand. As well as fish and coral, add shells, sea anemones, rocks, and pebbles.

Cane furniture has an underwater, plant-like feel, so it has been specially selected to go with the general theme.

The tongue-and-groove dresser painted a watery blue complements the underwater world depicted in the mural.

Wit & Daring

Experienced interior decorators often throw the rule book out the window to come up with something very different. This takes courage because it requires making a strong statement—which can be exciting, but can also go very wrong. There is no reason not to have a go—if you plan carefully and put together the design in a considered way, the results are usually very effective indeed. The key is to ensure that all the elements work together in a pleasing way and that the color scheme works well, too. Since the colors are affected by the natural light levels within a room, the only way to be sure of this is to try them out in the room (see page 35).

▲ Out of scale
A big G hardly seems the appropriate accessory for exquisite antique furniture. But it makes a statement, turning an ordinary sideboard into one with stacks of personality.

◄ A fine balance
Black, white, red, and yellow are a strong combination, but the real success is the balanced way in which everything is arranged.

▶ **Visual tricks**

Trompe l'oeil is a classic ploy for a witty
interior. These shelves filled with books are
actually a wallpaper design.

Living Dangerously

REFERENCE POINT

■ If fake fur skins for rugs aren't to your taste but you want to include a rug in your design, see pages 88–89 for other ideas.

■ Cushion covers needn't be made from fabric alone. Dress them up to match the style of your room. See pages 144–145 for ways to do this, and to find out what shapes of cushion are available to you.

Sometimes the simplest of ploys makes for an exciting interior. One classic idea is to use fake animal skins—fashionable through the ages, from Roman times to the present. Their appeal lies in the danger they symbolize of man confronting beast, and the sensual nature of the fur. Animal skins always make a strong statement: this person is no safe player.

Use animal skins as rugs on the floor, or on the wall as a decorative focal point. If the symbolism of animal slaughter that goes with even fake skins does not appeal, use animal-pelt-inspired printed fabrics instead, which will still add a strong design element to the room. Use them as cloths on tables, to upholster furniture, or as cushion covers. Animal prints tend to be fashion fabrics that are not always available, so if you see them, snap them up. They'll look wonderful made up into drapes or soft furnishings, and they won't look dated in the interior next year, or even in five years' time.

One of the reasons for animal prints' success is the fact that they all come in natural tones, so they look good with any color. Here, a zebra skin has been teamed with zingy lemon yellow and grass green to make a vibrant combination. An equally strong alternative would be tangerine and purple. However, you don't have to be limited to such colors when using animal prints—they also look good with neutrals and mid- and deep tones. (But they can overpower pastels.)

Another way to introduce a witty focal point in the room is to use an outstandingly lovely piece of furniture—a beautifully carved ethnic coffee table, perhaps, or an exquisite mirror. If it is outsized, so much the better, though this will need skillful handling. The item would need to be balanced by accessories that relate to its size—a pair of tall, slender table lamps, for example, paintings, or prints that can be grouped to set off the scale of the focal point. More ephemeral touches could be huge pieces of bamboo or stacks of sticks over six-feet tall, bound and strategically positioned. A simple vase of exotic flowers can also look striking. Try a few stems of bird-of-paradise, ginger, or curly, sprouting bamboo set in a tall, slim glass vase.

> Animal skins always make a strong statement: this person is no safe player.

ANIMAL PRINTS

Made by overprinting close-cropped fur with realistic-looking animal prints, fake furs are fabulous nowadays. What's more, the wonderful natural colors never look dated. Even now, when big game hunting is hardly politically correct, animal prints have a daring, cutting edge together with a truly funky feel.

Zebra is the all-time classic, which appeals because the dramatic stripes have a fluidity that swirl in various directions.

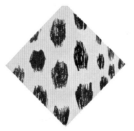

Cheetah is a much smaller motif, and appears more subtle. It is perfect for smaller rooms.

Giraffe has the same curious combination as zebra—geometric, yet changing in size and direction.

Cow is one of the boldest prints, evoking the Wild West. Yet the organic shapes have an appealing softness.

52

NOW LOOK AGAIN

Vibrant color schemes, especially when combined with black and white, always display boldness. Be daring and try one.

The beauty of animal skins is that almost any color complements the design. Here, emerald green looks truly striking next to zebra skin.

Large tropical flowers, set into a glass vase, make a strong statement that adds to the daring but can be easily altered.

Period Grandeur

In centuries past, when everything was made by hand, the very process of crafting, carving, and casting became an art form. There was time for attention to detail, and so detail flourished. Wonderful, nature-inspired forms of flowers and leaves, shells, and fruits seemed to grow out of the architecture, and grand houses were large enough to give space to the most intricate of designs. Given the legacy of such beautiful craftmanship, many owners of period houses love to replicate the look.

Although it can look overpowering in modern houses, period grandeur shouldn't be totally ruled out. A beautiful feature, such as an exquisitely carved piece of furniture or a glorious sparkling chandelier, can make a surprising but wonderful focal point in even the sleekest of modern loft apartments.

▲ Pleasing view

Architectural features, such as this curved alcove, add style to old houses. Its positioning provides a magnificent view from the hall.

◀ Classic blue

The tones of this period dining room immediately evoke the grandeur of yesteryear. The cornices and furniture have a Georgian feel, accentuated by the exquisite glass chandelier and the formal style of the table setting.

◀◀ Focus of attention

This magnificently carved wooden headboard would look impressive in any period home, from English high Victorian to Latin American estate. However, given enough ceiling height, it would also make a dramatic focal point in a modern loft apartment, where very little else would be needed in the room.

The Grand Salon

REFERENCE POINT

■ To find out more about making architectural details work well in your home, see pages 102–103.

■ Fireplaces are available in a great many styles. Information on what to choose—and how —is on pages 104–107.

■ Moldings can become very clogged with paint over the years. To find out about cleaning them, see pages 108–109.

For period grandeur to work, you need a large room, but this does not necessarily mean the style is limited to those who live in mansions. Even modest houses often have two reception rooms that can be opened up into a single, larger space. If the ceilings are high enough (at least eight feet), you have all the requirements to create your own grand salon—even if the rest of the house is more cozy.

The key to true period grandeur is architectural detail. Original fireplaces always make a focal point. If your fireplace is damaged, aim to restore rather than replace it; if it's been removed, replace it with as near to the original style as possible. Skirtings and cornices should be deep, and any ceiling molding or corbels restored. This basic architecture is the ideal backdrop for the grand, period style.

Authentic period decorating depends on very particular color schemes. This is because, until the twentieth century, paint shades were limited to natural pigments, which were usually drawn from local clays and plants. However, some tones were surprisingly strong. In Georgian times, it was not unusual to see rooms painted in vibrant yellows, deep reds, or any one of a range of blue-greens.

Windows were dressed in generous, floor-to-ceiling drapes, often swagged and trimmed with elaborate ribbons or fringing. The wider the window, the more swags could be incorporated, creating even more magnificent surroundings. Floors should be generally made of wood, stone, or ceramic, softened by some carpet squares or rugs—never wall-to-wall carpeting. For the look of period grandeur, use antique or reproduction furniture, which can span many styles. Choose from English polished mahogany, Shaker styles, painted Swedish, and elegant French Louis XV gilded pieces with cabriole legs. When choosing your furniture, look at proportion and detailing. If the pieces are in proportion with each other, both in size and in terms of bulk and detailing, they will sit happily together.

> In Georgian times, it was not unusual to see rooms painted in vibrant yellows, deep reds, or any one of a range of blue-greens.

PERIOD COLORS

The range of traditional paint shades used to be very limited compared with the thousands available since the introduction of chemical pigments. Falling mainly within four color groups (see right), the natural pigments, however, offered a pleasing finished effect. Many paint manufacturers have researched original paint colors, resulting in the authentic-color charts available today, which provide a perfect choice when decorating your home in the period style.

Traditional "whites" and stones seem murky to the modern eye, but they blend well with period hues.

Reds and earth shades have strong natural hues that were a popular choice for dining rooms.

Traditional blues and greens have a lot of gray in the mix, making them easy to live with and good for living rooms.

Yellows ranged from ocher to golden tones. Georgian living rooms were often decorated in the brightest of yellows.

NOW LOOK AGAIN

Generously swagged drapes turn the room into a grand salon. Celadon green was a great favorite in the early eighteenth century.

A cornice is essential for the period look. The cream ceiling is slightly lighter than the buttery yellow walls, making it look higher and grander.

The exposed legs of this chair have a feminine feel typical of the Georgian period. Later Victorian prudery dictated that chairs had "skirts."

Country Style

The fresh, relaxed look of country style gives it universal appeal and, although most of us see it as rooted in tradition, that does not mean that it never moves on. Just like any other style of decorating, country has evolved over the ages, reflecting the mood of the times. It is marked by several characteristics: the simple, robust style of furniture; the recurring, nature-inspired motifs; the country crafts, and the fresh color palette.

As long as you keep to these elements, you can be sure of a cohesive style that can be readily adapted to suit current tastes. Last year's drapes, for example, may still look gorgeous, but the whole room could be given a new look if you were to exchange yesteryear's tired-looking matching wallpaper for a clean coat of paint.

◀ All checked out

Checks are a classic country icon, giving a fresh and pretty look. The outsized buttercup yellow gingham used here has a contemporary slant, especially when set against the white tongue-and-groove cladding and white bedspreads.

 Quilt style

Quilts are one of the hallmarks of country style. Stitched together from old scraps of fabric to help their owners survive the rigors of the early winters, they have now become an art form, prized by many collectors.

▲ **Simple design**

This cream-painted traditional kitchen cupboard is classic country in design: practical, but nevertheless beautiful. The simple lines of country earthenware and china make these items the perfect subjects for display on the shelves. The whole ensemble makes a focal point to any country-style kitchen.

Country Bedroom

REFERENCE POINT

■ Color is clearly important to a country interior. Pages 32–35 discuss how to use color to maximum effect.

■ Fabric is also an essential element. For ideas about pattern, see below, and, for ways to use the fabric, see: Drapes (pages 124–127), Panels and Modern Curtains (pages 128–131), Soft Shades (pages 132–133), and Cushions and Throws (pages 144–145).

Pretty, yet unpretentious, country is the ultimate style for relaxed living. Everything has a natural balance that is easy on the eye and relaxed on display. Country style is certainly not minimal, but shelves are more likely to display a selection of household items than decorative trinkets. It's a look that survives a little disarray without the dusting demands of cluttered styles.

Country style is also appealing because it can easily be adapted as fashions change. Use color from the fresh country palette, take a lead from the typical fabric and furniture styles, introduce a hand-crafted element, and you're guaranteed that country look.

In the past, country colors were limited to traditional pigments taken from clays and plant materials, ranging from pink and terracotta earth shades through yellow ochers, olive tones, blues, and greens. Modern pigments offer much more choice, and the palette has lightened up, too, reflecting the colors of the countryside: bright blues, greens, reds, and yellows.

> Country style is appealing because it can be easily adapted as fashions change.

Country fabrics through the ages have been made from natural fibers, such as cotton, linen, or wool, and either woven into simple geometric designs, such as stripes, checks, or tartans, or printed with country motifs, such as flowers, farm animals, or pastoral scenes. Sometimes the fashion is for exuberant overall patterns, such as the country scenes on toile de Jouy or flamboyant florals. At other times, the country look can take on a more restrained personality, with roses that are rather more bud than blousy. Cabinet furniture is usually made from pine, which traditionally was either waxed or painted. Although paint can chip—and, indeed, frequently does—this is the more flexible option from a design standpoint because you can alter the colors as your tastes, or the fashions, change.

Country crafts are another element of the style. Add individual touches to your country interior with exquisite handmade, patchworked, and quilted comforters, tapestry cushions, and baskets created from willow or wire.

COUNTRY FABRICS

Fresh country fabrics are always woven from natural fibers: cotton, linen, or wool. Linen union, a combination of cotton and linen, is also a popular furnishing fabric because it combines the strength and weight of linen with the price advantages of cotton. Wool is used for blankets and rugs, often woven into tartan designs. Here are the popular themes for country designs.

Florals In addition to the more usual roses, common themes are wisteria, carnations, and chrysanthemums.

Gingham Most usually available in primary colors (red, yellow, and blue), but green and black are also popular.

Toile de Jouy This typical country-style pattern draws inspiration from its surroundings, often using fruit motifs.

Stripes Country kitchen linens were woven with colorful stripes, which have found their way into other rooms.

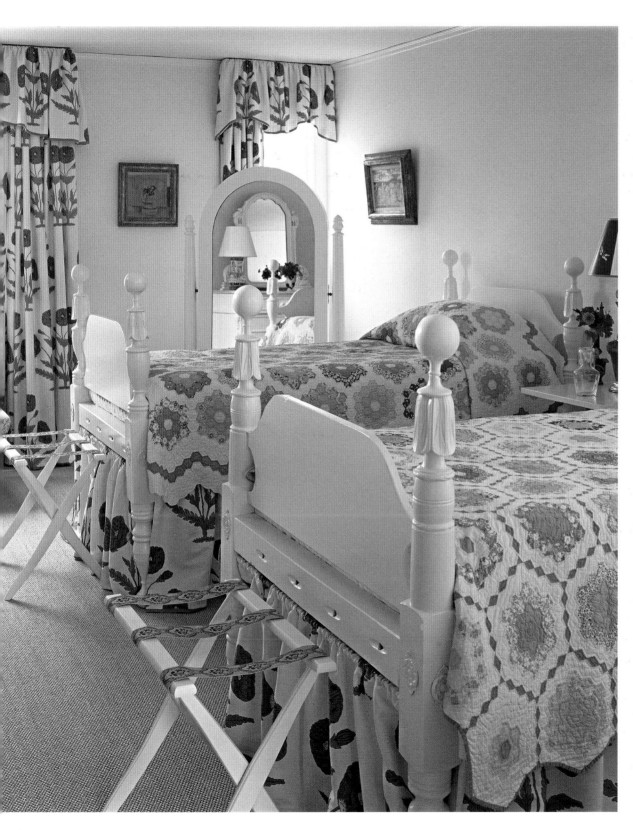

NOW LOOK AGAIN

A green-and-cream table lamp set between the two beds echoes some of the colors in the drapes and other furnishings.

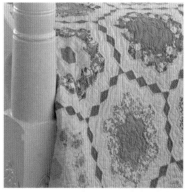

Patchwork is a country icon, and is a particularly effective way of bringing color and pattern into a room. It also makes any bed look most inviting.

Blue tulips with green leaves against a cream background create the perfect country bedroom fabric, used for drapes and bed valances.

Modern Living

Busy lives leave little time for clutter, so the clean, simple lines of modern interiors are a refreshing contrast to other, cozier spaces. Today's ability to live a more pared-down existence has partly been enabled by the introduction of central heating, air conditioning, and double glazing, dispensing with the need for draft-excluding heavy drapes and heat-preserving deep-pile carpets. Instead, sleek, long-lasting, and easy-to-maintain wooden floors have taken the place of wool underfoot. Simple translucent panels or even bare windows have replaced drapes to complement the smooth lines of unembellished modern interiors.

▲ Sleek kitchens

Shiny stainless steel brings light to modern kitchens, which are fast becoming the main living space in today's homes.

◀ Smooth lines

Cupboards, cleverly disguised as walls, offer plenty of storage space for hiding files, directories, and stationery.

▶ All white

Light-reflective and calming, white is the perfect backdrop to any room. Add color with bed linen, furniture, or accessories, or simply paint a vibrant panel on one wall.

Modern Bathroom

REFERENCE POINT

■ Your choice of faucets is an essential finishing touch. See bathroom faucets on pages 116–117 for more details on what is available.

■ Showers and basins are subsequently covered on pages 118–121.

■ For information on towel racks and other forms of heating in the bathroom, see pages 112–113.

Bathrooms have fast become the home equivalent of modern luxury spas. It was not so long ago that a single bathroom was squeezed into the smallest room in the house. Modern builders aim to include at least two in every home, and, ideally, one per bedroom. And, while this is the room in which we want to luxuriate and relax, it's also the room that needs to be kept scrupulously clean.

Today's homeowners seek clinically clean wipe-down surfaces yet lots of ambience; great light, but plenty of privacy; and generous showering, washing, and bathing space—all packed into what is often the smallest room in the house. It's a tall order and one that leaves no surprise that this, in terms of dollars per square foot, can easily be the most expensive room in the house.

For your modern bathroom, look to incorporate a boxed-in bath, a wipe-clean surface with an inset basin, and plenty of closet space for all the less glorious bathroom paraphernalia.

If possible, make the shower a walk-in space rather than incorporating it over the bath. And, if space does not allow for both shower and bath, then it's the bath that is most likely to go. An efficient shower with plenty of room to move in is more compatible with the wash-and-go modern lifestyle than a soak in the bath. Besides, with builders allowing for more wash areas, there should be room for the bath elsewhere in your home.

Designers have many tricks to bring extra natural light into rooms throughout the house, one being the use of glass bricks. Use these in addition to, or instead of, windows to allow light in from the outside, or use them in a wall shared with the corridor to "borrow light" from other parts of the house. If you want to be sure of your privacy, fix them at higher-than eye level. Within the bathroom itself, use glass bricks as a screen to section off areas, such as the shower, while still allowing the light through.

> Designers now have many tricks to bring extra natural light into rooms throughout the house, one being the use of glass bricks.

WALL TILES

A water-resistant backsplash around the bathtub and basin is essential, and ceramic or stone tiles still offer one of the most efficient and popular solutions. There is a very wide choice of plain and printed ceramic tiles, in sizes that range from tiny mosaic to 1' 6" x 2' giants. In addition to the common ceramic type, tiles are available in different materials and shapes (see wall tiles on pages 98–99).

Glass mosaics bring light to the walls. The adhesive darkens the color, so bear this in mind when choosing.

Round mosaics add witty interest to the bathroom. They are supplied on a net backing and are simple to fit to the wall.

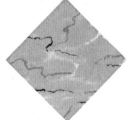

Marble tiles are a restrained and calming feature in the modern bathroom. The available colors are surprisingly varied.

Limestone makes a light, easy-to-live-with surface that can be used as wall tiles and as a wash basin surface.

NOW LOOK AGAIN

A glass-brick wall can let light in from the outside, or from other areas in the house.

Inset basins make for easy-to-wipe surfaces. This one was made in a single piece from a high-density synthetic resin.

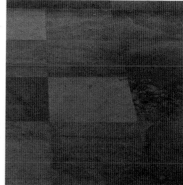

Slate, with its naturally cracked surface, is the ideal bathroom floor material. It is nonslip, waterproof, and simple to keep clean.

Seaside Style

The wonderful weathered tones of driftwood, pebbles, sand, and shells, conjuring up relaxed days on the beach, make seaside style irresistible. The clean simplicity of bleached wood against pure white and deck-chair stripes, teamed with marine blue and the classic seaside motifs of fish and shells, creates an enduring look that's simple to achieve.

Essentially relaxed, seaside style makes for easy family living and has universal appeal that has stood the test of time. Keep the look for your summer home by the sea, or try it in the watery ambience of the bathroom, where shells can be used as soap dishes or lined up in serried ranks for a sculptural display.

▶ Sea bathing

Fresh, white-painted bathrooms, accessorized with seaside articles, look good both in vacation homes and back in the city.

▼ Sea view

Beach house rooms are often small, so use white paint to visually enlarge them and unify the uneven surfaces of rafters and walls.

Seaside Bedroom

REFERENCE POINT

■ Once you have gathered together all your seaside memorabilia, you will want to display them to their best effect. See pages 158–159 for some tips.

■ There is a wide choice of types of paint available. So before searching for the right white, read the advice on pages 94–95 first.

The seaside look is second cousin to country style. Pure, natural fabrics, usually cotton, are common to both, either printed, or woven into geometric stripes. They are both essentially unpretentious, but the seaside look, if anything, is more pared back. Simplicity is all, and one of the ways to unify disparate surfaces is to get busy with a large pot of white paint. Seaside cabins are often made of timber, and it is easy to re-create this look elsewhere with tongue-and- groove cladding. The whole lot can be painted white, along with any furniture. This has the two advantages of offering a clean canvas against which seaside elements can be displayed, and creating a sense of space. It also allows you to pick up inexpensive pieces of junk-shop furniture, which can quickly be brought into line with the unifying white. Take a tip from the Mediterranean, and keep seaside style looking pristine by freshening up your room with a new touch of white paint every spring.

> One of the greatest joys of seaside style is the opportunity it provides for incorporating your family's own seaside memorabilia.

The classic seaside color scheme is white and blue, and while it complements the weathered tones of driftwood and pebbles, there is no reason to stick slavishly to this. Here, the soft furnishings are in a country pink, but the overall look is just as effective.

For the floors, natural wood or stone is the best solution, softened by simple woven rugs (ideally given a nautical theme, such as ropes or life preservers). One of the greatest joys of seaside style is the opportunity it provides for incorporating all your family's own seaside memorabilia. Use piles of the very best shells, pebbles, and even ammonites, lovingly collected from the beach over successive visits; glorious pieces of driftwood, weathered, sculpted and bleached by season upon season of salty waves and baking sun. As well as Nature's accessories, there are many more seaside motifs that add to the style: brightly painted miniature beach huts or sailboats, fishermen's nets, and sea birds, all of which can be used to adorn windowsills, shelves, and fireplaces.

MARINE THEMES

The seaside is a treasury of motifs that are both evocative and easy to copy. Display the genuine articles collected from the beach, or look for printed fabrics, paintings, or photographs that feature seaside themes; then turn them into drapes or cushions. If you're feeling creative, paint, draw, or stencil images onto pieces of furniture, fabric, or lampshades to create your own seaside hideaway.

Pebbles come in glorious colors. Search out special ones with stripes running through to make an interesting collection.

Shells You won't find a nautilus shell like this on the beach, but shells make exquisite accessories.

Fishy shapes are easy to paint freehand. If you're feeling ambitious, try the ever-appealing seahorse.

Starfish have a pleasing symmetrical shape, making them perfect for wallpaper, curtain, or bed-linen patterns.

NOW LOOK AGAIN

By painting everything white, including curtain rods and rings, shelves, and bed frames, you can quickly create a sense of unity and space in your seaside room.

Simple woven fabrics incorporating fresh red or blue stripes have the requisite clean seaside feel.

If you want to introduce printed designs, choose simple country styles, such as this floral fabric.

Swedish Style

Traditional Swedish style, also called Gustavian style, with its pretty, painted furniture and distinctive color palette of whites, creams, greens, and blues, has enduring charm. Dating back to the reign of Gustav III, the subtly carved furniture shapes betray their elegant eighteenth-century roots, which is when the style first became popular. Paint is applied to many different surfaces—furniture, walls, and sometimes floors—bringing a calming, cohesive feel to a room, while making good use of any available natural light (which is of prime importance in the light-deprived Scandinavian winters). This concern with natural light has subsequently become a modern priority and, perversely, gives this eighteenth-century style fresh new appeal.

▲ Decorative warmth

Tiled or enameled wood-burning stoves are typical of traditional Swedish style. Although large, they can make a highly decorative feature in a room.

◄ Color perfection

Pretty pastel colors are the hallmark of Swedish style. They work because they are softened with gray for a restful, harmonious scheme.

► Blue tile style

More usually associated with Dutch Delft tiles, this blue and white combination was very popular in Europe in the early eighteenth century, due to the mass introduction of Chinese designs. This is echoed here by the display of Chinese ginger jars on the shelves. The shapely chairs are more typical of Swedish style.

Swedish Dining Room

REFERENCE POINT

■ With carefully grouped lights and the use of dimmer switches, it is possible to evoke the romance of candlelight using electric light. See pages 146–153 for solutions.

■ Although limewash would have been the original paint of choice, today's range of flat paints has a very similar effect. See pages 94–95 for further information.

Swedish style translates well in the dining room because carved wooden furniture was the great Swedish strength, even spilling over into the sitting room as cushioned benches. There is a wide range of pretty wooden dining chairs to choose from and, painted white, the reproductions look every bit as good as the originals. Traditionally, the seats were softened with small cushion pads, often frilled around the edges and tied into position. Here, the cushions are all white, but fresh cotton ginghams in red, yellow, or green, or heavy linens, perhaps featuring a single central stripe in blue or in red, would be equally as much in keeping.

Traditionally, all the furniture—table, chairs, dressers, and shelves—would have been painted in colors that range from creams and whites to gray-blues and gray-greens. These gentle shades were very effective in the soft light of northern latitudes, adding an airy feel to rooms, which, certainly in winter, had very few hours of sunshine. The original paints would have contained lime,

which lent a chalkiness and luminosity, and there are now several paint companies that supply this traditional style of paint. But whether you use these or their modern equivalents, when painted on walls, furniture, and even floors, the overall effect is one of cohesiveness combined with a general feeling of space and calm.

Accessories in the Swedish dining room would tend to be functional—dressers laden with china and glass, water jugs, and a great many candlesticks or lanterns. The seemingly endless dark winter nights led to the Swedish tradition of using myriad candles at every opportunity and while, with the introduction of electric light, that no longer holds the same importance as it did in years past, the effect of their dancing flames is still magical. They are particularly lovely when set in glass lanterns or holders that reflect and magnify the light. When setting the table, choose low candleholders to ensure the flames will be well below eye level, so as not to interrupt the flow of conversation.

> The gentle colors that epitomize Swedish style were very effective in the soft light of northern latitudes.

SWEDISH COLOR SCHEMES

The blues, greens, and grays of the typical Swedish color scheme are very close to each other in the spectrum, creating a harmonious effect. However, it is also typically Swedish to introduce accent colors on fabrics that are considerably brighter: red, royal blue, green, and pink.

Whites, off-whites, and creams are very popular in Swedish style, and provide the basis for many schemes.

Soft gray-blues are often known as Gustavian colors, acknowledging their roots in the time of Gustav III.

Flashes of color are typically geometric: ginghams, window checks, and stripes.

Greens can be a little stronger, but they retain a good proportion of gray, providing a typical softness.

72

NOW LOOK AGAIN

White plates on a white plate rack make a decorative detail on the walls that is offset by the simple lines of the hanging glass lantern.

A simple flower arrangement is all that is needed for table decoration. Seasonal blooms always work well with unpretentious Swedish style.

Swedish dining chair cushions traditionally had frilled "skirts"—a look that is still soft, feminine, and does not become outdated.

Absolute
Essentials

Floors

Since they are part of the architecture of the house, choose solid floors for their enduring style, not to make a fashion statement.

◄ Naturally wood

Wood has been used for flooring throughout the centuries in many parts of the world. Although it was traditionally oiled or polished, nowadays we're more likely to choose a hardwearing varnish that offers a beautiful sheen, but requires a lot less maintenance.

◄◄ Rug style

Before the advent of fitted carpets, carpet squares were laid on top of polished wood floors or linoleum. This is less usual today, although the trend is more for smaller, easy-to-clean rugs to be laid onto hard floors. This cream runner is both light and elegant, and soft under foot.

◄◄ Natural choice

Very hardwearing, natural fibers, such as coir, jute, and seagrass, are increasing in popularity. This coir flooring looks just right in a country-style bedroom.

◄◄◄ Pattern interest

Simple geometric patterns can be introduced with the use of wood stains. Here, a contrasting border running around the room finishes it off stylishly and is not difficult to do, using masking tape to keep the lines perfect. Apply the stain before sealing the floor.

Stone

This ancient flooring material still holds much appeal. Original stone floors add character to old houses, and new stone brings confidence to modern homes. When looking for a suitable flooring for your home, it's best to choose a stone that is traditionally used in your area, and it is especially important to use local stone at ground level where the indoors and outdoors converge.

The installation of a solid stone floor is a skilled job, which requires preparation of a subfloor and skilled laying. So hire a professional to get it done properly.

78

COLOR AND TEXTURE

■ **Limestone** has a fine texture and a range of colors from sandy tones to grays and browns. It comes from sedimentary rock, and is often faintly patterned by the fossilized remains of marine creatures. It is available either dressed (smooth) or with a more rugged, cracked surface.

■ **Granite** is harder than limestone, being an igneous rock formed under heat and pressure. Colors range from near-black and dark green to pale grays and creams. Granite sometimes includes sparkling quartzes and feldspars.

■ **Marble** is the hardest stone of all, formed by the recrystallization of limestone, which results in wonderful pale cream- and gray-veined stone.

■ **Slate,** in charcoal grays, deep greens, blues, and browns, is a very hard, igneous stone, and can have a naturally nonslip, cracked surface. It is inexpensive and classy.

◄ **Original beauty**
Flagstone floors have been a country favorite for centuries and, indeed, some farmhouses still have their original floors. Usually made of local stone, they have a timeless integrity that looks good even in a modern farmhouse.

▶ **Sophisticated slate**
The elegant gray tone of slate has made it a popular choice for modern stone floors. These slate tiles have been dressed, giving them a smooth surface.

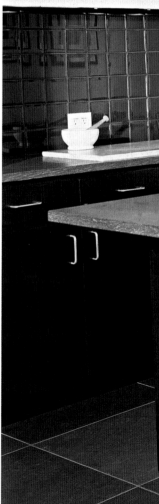

Ceramic Tiles

Less expensive than stone, although almost as durable, ceramic floor tiles are manufactured to regular sizes of different dimensions and can be used to create a variety of looks, from elegantly plain to intricately patterned.

They are available either in their natural state (as quarry or terracotta tiles, for example) for a rustic look, or glazed (offering a huge range of colors from subtle neutrals to vibrant brights). Fully waterproof, glazed ceramic tiles are an especially popular choice for bathrooms and shower-room floors, although they are also suitable for halls and kitchens. In hot countries, they are very often used throughout the house, as they are cool underfoot and easy to maintain.

UNGLAZED OR GLAZED?

■ **Natural terracotta and quarry tiles** are made from unglazed, baked clay. If left unsealed, they will quickly stain. The supplier will suggest a suitable sealer. If the tiles have not been waterproofed, they can be sealed with a polyurethane varnish. A traditional seal is one part linseed oil with one part turpentine.

■ **Glazed or unglazed ceramic tiles** come in a wide range of sizes and shapes. Choose large, uniform tiles for a sleek modern look, or make up patterns using color or combining different shapes, such as lozenges and squares, hexagons, triangles, and rectangles.

■ **Mosaic tiles** can be made of ceramic, glass, or marble. Use a single size and color for a modern look, or make up an elaborately patterned floor using several different colors.

◀ **Natural choice**
Terracotta tiles, with their natural tones and handmade appearance, look wonderful in rustic kitchens. Warmer underfoot than glazed ceramics, they are a traditional choice, especially in cooler climates.

◀◀ **Check mate**
Ceramic tiles make the ideal bathroom or shower-room floor, being waterproof, resilient, and easy to clean. This pale blue and black checker design makes a pretty alternative to the more usual black and white.

Wood

The glorious natural tones of wooden floors improve with time, even benefiting visually from the wear and tear of age. Whatever you choose (see opposite), no floorboard takes too kindly to stiletto heels, as they quickly dent the floor. The same goes for weight-bearing, slim-legged furniture, so make sure it has rubber tips, or buy special protectors.

Each timber has its own natural tone. Ash, beech, and maple are the palest, followed by midtoned oak and deeper-toned cherry, mahogany, and various tropical woods (the darkest being ebony, which is virtually black). Try to go for what was originally in your home or area; if in doubt, install classic oak, which offers a pleasing midtone.

▶ Paint perfection

Painting the floor is an ideal way to spruce up old floorboards inexpensively. Sand the floor and give it two undercoats. You can use gloss or matte eggshell paint, but hardwearing floor paint is more durable. If you use eggshell, apply a final coat of matte seal for protection.

▼ Painted style

If you're tired of your old wood floor, simply sand it down and paint it in any pattern you want. This tiled look is achieved using masking tape to mask off the squares. It requires meticulous measuring, and should be finished with three coats of varnish. Before starting work, ensure the paint and varnish are compatible by testing on a spare piece of wood.

SOLID WOOD AND VENEER

■ **Before deciding on a wood**, bear in mind that hardwood is a lot more resilient than soft. The length of time it looks good also depends on the quality of varnish with which it is finished. There is also a choice to be made between floorboards and tongue-and-groove flooring.

■ **Traditional floorboards** were literally simple wooden boards that were nailed or screwed into the joists, which often left small drafty gaps between them. When refurbishing original floorboards, experts usually lift them, cut out any damage, and re-lay them closer together. The sawdust from the sanding is swept into the gaps before sealing, thus reducing any drafts.

■ **Tongue-and-groove planks** also form solid wood flooring materials and fit together without leaving gaps. The wider and longer boards are generally more expensive. Some have beveled edges for an elegant finish. When buying, check that the tongue is far enough below the surface to allow for future sandings when refurbishing the floor.

■ **Strip flooring** is made up of lots of smaller and thinner strips of hardwood veneered onto tongue-and-groove softwood. This is less expensive than a solid wood floor. Check the thickness of the veneer to allow for future sanding.

■ **Prefinished boards** come with a factory-finished varnish, which means you can save money on the labor costs of sealing the floor.

Semihard Flooring

Available in sheet or tile form, most semihard flooring first appeared in the twentieth century. Offering a soft, waterproof surface, it is relatively inexpensive and easy to lay, and so became a practical, popular choice, especially for kitchens and bathrooms. Most forms of semihard flooring are made in a wide range of colors, which means it is an ideal fashion flooring. But ironically, older flooring materials such as linoleum and rubber, which have become more popular since the turn of the millennium, are both more expensive than other forms of sheet flooring and require professional installation.

▶ Sheet treat

Sheet vinyl became a popular twentieth-century kitchen flooring. Inexpensive and easy to lay, it is a simple DIY job. Designs often mimic classic tiles and so suit many styles of kitchen.

▼ On the tiles

Vinyl tiles are ideal for a bathroom. They're fully waterproof, not too cold underfoot, and wash down quickly and easily. This pale blue and white checker design makes a pretty alternative to the more usual classic black and white.

VERSATILE FINISHES

■ **Vinyl** was the wonder flooring of the 1950s. Easy to lay, it is available in a multitude of designs, which are very often a copy of more traditional floors.

■ **Linoleum** has now freed itself of its dowdy postwar image. This totally natural material, made from a compound that includes linseed, cork, and resin, now comes in a wide range of colors. It is easily cut and can be used to make up interesting and varied floor designs.

■ **Rubber** has a modern edge with industrial appeal. Available either with a smooth finish or in a range of studded styles, it can be custom-made in any color you like. Not inexpensive, it should be laid professionally, after which the initial manufacturer's coating should be stripped off and a new coating applied.

■ **Cork** was very popular in the 1970s, and its natural tones are still appealing. Available in tile form, it is easy to lay, inexpensive, and resilient.

Carpets

Soft underfoot and available in almost any color and texture you want, wall-to-wall carpeting became the postwar byword for interior luxury. Carpets not only looked good, but their deep, woolly pile acted as a form of insulation, keeping cold houses cozy in the winter. Vacuuming kept them clean and was far less time consuming than the alternative of floor polishing and the beating that rugs required.

Although interior tastes have moved on, and carpets don't enjoy quite the popularity of previous decades, they are still an obvious choice for bedrooms, where barefoot comfort is all and the chance of staining is minimal.

IT'S QUALITY THAT COUNTS

■ **Wool carpet** is warm, soft, and stain resistant, and although one of the most expensive fibers, is long lasting and retains its good looks. Many wool carpets contain nylon for extra strength—80% wool, 20% nylon is the most popular mix.

■ **Acrylic** is the nearest man-made equivalent to wool, though cheaper and quicker to soil. However, it is easy to clean.

■ **Nylon** flattens more easily than wool.

■ **Density of pile** is an indication of carpet quality. The denser the pile, the less likely it is to flatten and the longer it is likely to last. Check the density by bending back a carpet sample to see how closely the tufts are positioned.

■ **Underlay** is essential if you want to get good wear out of the carpet. Some come with an integral foam back. Hessian-backed carpet has to be laid on top of a separate felt or rubber underlay.

◀ **Pattern perfection**
Modern carpet patterns are more likely to be neatly geometric than swirly and floral. This restrained taupe and cream diamond design is both elegant and soft underfoot, making it perfect for a bedroom.

▶ **Cream dream**
Light-colored carpets, like this one, help to introduce an airy feel to the whole room, especially if the walls are painted to match. This deep-pile carpet adds a sense of luxury to a stylish bedroom.

Rugs

Rugs have had a renaissance. By the end of the twentieth century, carpet lost favor to sleeker wood flooring due to the combination of a distaste for the house dust mites that thrived in its pile and stain-removing difficulties. Also, with the advent of central heating, there was no longer a need for the insulating quality of carpet. However, we still love a little softness underfoot, and rugs are the highly manageable solution.

Along with the return of traditional rugs to furnish a floor, new rugs have also found a place, and they are often chosen to make a bold statement.

A WORLD TOUR

■ **Contemporary rugs** are usually deep piled, brightly colored, and feature abstract patterns. They come in many shapes.

■ **Kelims** from Turkey and Iran are made as a tapestry of thick wool.

■ **Dhurries** are handwoven cotton rugs from India. They come in a wide choice of colors and designs, and large retailers commission designs to suit modern tastes.

■ **Caucasian and Turkish** rugs are associated with the Orient. There are many types. Kazaks have large, geometric designs. Soumacs are flat woven, often with diamond designs. Shirvans have small geometric patterns and a short pile.

■ **Aubusson rugs** from France often feature floral designs, and antique examples can fetch very large sums of money.

■ **Chinese rugs** are deep piled and richly colored, featuring traditional Chinese motifs.

◄ Rug art
Boldly colored and abstractly patterned rugs can make a dramatic statement in living areas. Set in a room furnished in white, this fuchsia square rug teams with the blue and yellow wall paintings as a piece of interior art.

◄◄ Faded glory
Traditional Turkish rugs have never fallen from favor. There are plenty of new ones to choose from, but antique examples have a beauty all their own because the tones of the natural dyes have softened exquisitely with time.

Natural Choice

Sleek, neutral, and textured, natural fiber flooring is fast becoming a designer favorite. For a long time associated with utility flooring, it now comes latex-backed for laying throughout the house and features interesting bouclé, herringbone, and basket-weave textures. It is not easy to lay, and carpet fitters will still try to dissuade you from choosing it, but once down, it is both more resilient and stain resistant than carpet. The colors range from pale biscuit and honey to mahogany, and some incorporate red, green, or indigo strands within the weave.

▶ Just jute

The softest underfoot of the natural fibers, jute is the best choice for bedrooms. Here, its natural tones blend in perfectly with the neutral color scheme of its surroundings.

▼ Sensational sisal

Natural sisal teams well with almost any color scheme. Here, it blends in with the wooden dining table, making a cohesive block of color to set against the wine-red walls.

A CHOICE OF TEXTURE

■ **Jute** was traditionally reserved for making sacking, rope, and carpet backing. It is the softest and most popular of the natural floor coverings.

■ **Sisal** is resilient and versatile, possibly the most popular of the natural fibers, being suitable for stairways, halls and landings, living and dining rooms, and bedrooms.

■ **Coir** is traditionally used for door mats and is a little prickly underfoot. It is inclined to be chunkier and less refined than sisal.

■ **Seagrass** comes in soft, natural tones, often tinged with green. Its slightly sheeny surface, which is naturally stain resistant, makes it a practical flooring choice. However, it can be rather slippery, and so shouldn't be used on the stairs.

90

Wall Finishes

If walls are in good condition and properly prepared, their look can be changed relatively quickly and easily.

▲ Color statement

Strong red looks stylish and contemporary, and beautifully sets off a wall of pictures. It provides an ideal background for the streamlined modern furnishings.

◀ White difference

These simple, rectangular wall tiles take on an interesting look when designed in a brick bond style. They work particularly well here, as they echo the simple rectangular form of the ceramic Belfast sink.

◀◀ Country cheer

Gingham immediately gives a country feel, so this yellow checked wallpaper is the perfect starting point for a fresh, spring-like bedroom.

Paints

For instant color impact, paint is hard to beat. Given the starting point of a well-prepared wall, it is quick and easy to apply, relatively inexpensive, and easy to maintain. Modern formulations offer a range of colors that stretches into the thousands, and computer-aided mixing machines can even color-match fabric swatches. Choosing colors can be deceptive, however, since paint swatches are small, set against a brilliant white background, and often viewed under fluorescent light, which is likely to be very different from the ambient light of your room. (To help you make the right choice, see pages 32–35.)

There are many ways to use paint color. You can paint the whole room, woodwork and all, in the same shade, to provide a clean background for furnishings and accessories, or you can use it to create a range of different effects and patterns. Stencils and stamps are an easy way to bring pattern to the walls, or you can create geometric designs, such as stripes, circles, or checkerboards in contrasting colors.

94

▲ Clever checks

Cream and white squares create a subtle checkerboard effect on the walls of this elegant sitting room. A diagonal of black squares on one wall introduces a touch of energetic contrast.

◀ Bright idea

Buttercup yellow is always a happy color and will lift your spirits every morning when you wake up. A matching shade of yellow on walls and woodwork is the perfect sunny background for this bedroom.

◀◀ Blue mood

A strong color statement can be taken a step further by painting all the surfaces in the same shade, including walls, skirtings, baseboards, and picture rails. Although bold, it offers a calm, harmonious look, unbroken by the woodwork, which is more usually painted white, which can be distracting.

WHICH PAINT TO USE?

■ **Latex paint** is water based and used for walls and ceilings. Modern compounds incorporate brighteners for a huge range of clear colors, and vinyl for an easy-to-apply, hardwearing finish. It is available in matte, eggshell, and silk.

■ **Liquid gloss** is the professionals' oil-based choice, providing a shiny, extra-hardwearing finish for woodwork and metal.

■ **Oil-based nondrip gloss** is easier to use than liquid gloss and has become a DIY favorite.

■ **Eggshell or satin** gives a flatter look than gloss, but is nevertheless hardwearing enough for woodwork and metal.

■ **Primer** is used to seal bare surfaces such as wood, metal, and plaster before painting with oil-based paints.

■ **Undercoat** provides a stable, opaque base for some gloss paints. Check product packaging instructions for preparation and application of your chosen finish.

■ **Varnish** gives a transparent, glossy finish for woodwork, to protect it while enhancing its natural grain.

■ **Special-effect paints** include softening or overglaze, metallic and pearly finishes, and translucent washes for woodwork.

■ **Traditional finishes** include soft (nonwashable) and casein (wipeable) distempers, used for a soft, chalky look.

95

Papers

The easiest way to introduce pattern to your walls is with wallpaper. Within hours, bold stripes, traditional florals, or great swathes of imitation paint effects can be transforming the room. They can be matched, coordinated with, or contrasted to, fabrics in the room. Generally, the stronger the pattern you use on the wall, the cozier the overall effect will be and the less you will need in terms of pictures and accessories.

One of the advantages of wallpaper is that you can see just what shade the finished color will be, as opposed to paint, which dries darker and can be difficult to assess. This is crucial if you plan a special effect, such as sponging or rag rolling, that is made up of several layers of different colors. With wallpaper, what you see is what you get.

DIFFERENT MATERIALS, DIFFERENT EFFECTS

■ **Papers** are the traditional wall coverings, and still have a luxury feel. The heavier the paper, the better the quality. Many are printed with designs that echo the original woodblock method of printing, but many contemporary designs are also available.

■ **Lining papers** are used to prepare walls both for paint and for paper. When papering over lining paper, the lining should be hung horizontally to avoid a clashing of seams.

■ **Paper-backed vinyl** wall coverings are often easier to hang than their all-paper cousins. They are also more hardwearing and have a wipe-clean surface.

■ **Blown vinyl** incorporates interesting textures into vinyl designs.

■ **Relief wallpapers,** which are designed to be painted, are traditionally used in busy traffic areas, such as in halls, below the dado, for protection against heavy wear.

■ **Photographic reproduction** is a new development with dramatic results. Any image, including family photographs, can be reproduced as wallpaper panels. Make a feature of it by putting it up on one wall only and painting the others.

◀ Bold stripes

Use bold stripes judiciously. In a large room like this, they make a confident statement and perfectly set off the large paintings. In a smaller room, they could be overbearing. The key is scale. As a guideline, make sure that at least ten stripes of each color will fit across the width of the room. Fine stripes create an altogether different effect, as they have a subtle, broken-up, allover look.

▼ Team spirit

Pretty prints are a traditional country favorite, providing an atmosphere of cozy intimacy. Many manufacturers produce coordinated ranges of fabrics and wallpapers that can be mixed and matched for an individual look. Here, a fine, busy country floral has been teamed with bold window checks. The white of the bedding adds a crisp touch, setting off the pattern all around it.

Wall Tiles

Dating back to pre-Roman times, wall tiles make an attractive, waterproof surface that's particularly useful in bathrooms and kitchens. There are many types (see below), but that's just the beginning of the design opportunities.

Given the same tiles, you can create very different looks, depending on the colors you choose, the way you use the varying shapes, the way they are arranged on the wall, and the color of the grout you select. For example, some tiles come as squares, hexagons, lozenges, rectangles, and triangles, which can be jigsawed together to make interesting, unusual designs. Typical examples of these are traditional English tessellated designs or Mexican clay tile designs.

Rectangular tiles can be arranged in neat rows, or as brick bonding. Square tiles can take on a very different look if they are arranged diagonally, rather than in the regular row-upon-row fashion. However, they will require much more cutting to fit.

VARIATIONS IN SIZE AND SHAPE

■ **Glazed ceramic tiles** are resilient, waterproof, and hardwearing, and come in a wide variety of shapes, colors, and sizes, ranging from 4-inch squares to 12-inch squares and more. They are individually glued into position, and the grout is applied once the adhesive is dry.

■ **Mosaic tiles** can be made from stone, ceramic, or glass. Each individual tile is small, but they are supplied grouped together on mesh, ready spaced for easy application. Most are square, but round and random pebble shapes are also available.

■ **Mirror tiles** can be used to good effect to reflect light and make a space seem larger.

■ **Printed tiles** are made in many patterns and colors, ranging from intricate Victorian designs to bold motifs. They can be used to cover a whole wall, or teamed with coordinating plain tiles.

■ **Stone tiles** can be made from marble, limestone, or granite. They are sometimes "tumbled" for a softer effect, giving them slightly rounded edges and corners.

▲ **Elegant solution**
Natural limestone, cut into large tiles, makes for an elegant modern bathroom. Here they have been attached to the walls as well as laid on the floors for an all-around unity. If you live in a cold climate, install underfloor heating.

98

▲ Small charm

Four-inch ceramic tiles add interest to kitchen walls and work especially well if the units are sleek and unembellished. These tiles show natural variation in color, giving a sense of depth to the whole design.

◄ Feature wall

Mosaic tiles on just one bathroom or shower-room wall always make an interesting feature. As well as introducing color to the room, they set off fixtures, such as this elegant wall-mounted basin.

Architectural Details

A building's quality comes down to detail, which lies in careful selection—and meticulous workmanship.

▲ Strong choice

Halls were often paneled to baseboard level to protect them against what can be hard wear. Many were left with a natural wood finish; this paneling looks refreshing when painted white.

◀ Shiny solution

Faucets can be used for architectural detail. Here, two elegant chrome spouts look striking in a modern kitchen.

◀◀ Top style

Victorian houses invariably had cornices; the grander ones had molding across the ceiling, too, bringing a sense of quality to the room.

◀◀◀ Focal point

A stunning carved-panel chimneypiece sets the style for this exquisite period room. Painted in deep cream, it is made even more of a feature against the café au lait walls.

The Details that Count

When it comes to interiors, attention to detail cannot be under-estimated. Architectural elements that are focal points, such as fireplaces, obviously make an instant impression, but others, which might seem insignificant, can turn an ugly duckling of a room into a truly beautiful one, and vice versa. The Victorians understood this well and paid a lot of attention to creating well-proportioned windows, elaborate cornices and corbels, deep skirting boards, and pretty fireplaces.

Sadly, over the years, "renovations" have sometimes stripped houses of these, often to their detriment. Even twentieth-century houses, with their more subtle architectural detailing, can be made or broken by renovations. Low ceilings can be rendered plain by the removal of even humble cornices, and the visual proportions of rooms can be changed by the size of the skirtings.

Whether architectural detail is likely to complement or ruin an interior comes down to two factors: first, whether it is appropriate for the period and style of the house and second, whether or not the proportions are correct. Getting the first right is not too difficult, as there are often clues within the building—you may find the last vestiges of a cornice, for example. Alternatively, you could ask to look in a neighbor's house or research the style of buildings at the time your home was built. Getting the proportions right can be more elusive and is a skill that is acquired by looking at similar buildings. But applying common sense always helps. If you have large rooms and high ceilings, the architectural detail can be more generous, and vice versa for small and low spaces.

▶ ▲ Right lights
Dramatic light fixtures are like functional sculptures, and so can be used to make a statement. Make an even stronger statement by hanging a pair, as here, above the workstation.

▶ Accentuate the positive
Finely detailed cornices look wonderful painted in crisp white, especially when set off by boldly colored walls, such as this classic terra-cotta.

▶▶ Clear winner
If you have beautiful architecture, don't cover it up. These elegant windows with fine architraves are best left visible rather than shrouded by drapes.

Fireplaces

For centuries, the fireplace reigned supreme as the focal point of the room. Visually, it provided the most prominent architectural detail, and the heat and dancing flames offered incentive enough for everyone to be drawn to the fireside. But that was before the advent of television and central heating. Regrettably, as these began to have an impact on our lives in the twentieth century, home owners raced to rip out or cover up what they perceived as dirty and labor-intensive heat sources, thus stripping their homes of much of their character. The error is now being redressed, and fireplaces are reclaiming their importance as architectural focal points within the room.

The choices are myriad, but first decide whether you are going to look at period or contemporary designs. You can then address more-specific design requirements (see pages 106–107).

▲ Modern movement
Clean, simple, and modern hole-in-the-wall fireplaces can range from a floor-to-ceiling design to a much more modest opening, like this. It can be an inexpensive option where a period fireplace is beyond repair.

◀ Wood works
This beautiful, unembellished, modern wooden fireplace surround looks lovely in light maple, especially when complemented by cream marble slips.

▶ All bright and beautiful
Yellow and white tiles laid in a checkerboard pattern give this period fireplace a contemporary slant. The design works because the surround is left intact and the tiles simply replace more fancy Victorian originals.

A FIREPLACE FOR ALL TASTES

■ **If you have a period home,** you may want to reinstate a period fireplace. If you can't find an original one at a reasonable price, look for a reproduction, many of which are made using traditional molds.

■ **Contemporary fireplaces** have moved on with new, very different designs, introducing a lively feature to modern interiors. Some are still designed to burn wood or solid fuel; others, of both period and modern styles, have gas flames.

■ **The most recent designs** of gas fires don't even pretend to be real. Instead of "logs" or "coals," they "burn" fireproof, reconstructed beach pebbles, driftwood, architectural stone details, or even simple shapes, like pyramids, spheres, and cubes.

■ **Fireplaces have shrunk** to holes in walls, become the focal point in fireside bench seating, and are raised on surfaces within fire openings. The modern applications continue to grow.

Medieval stone fireplace

This large, open stone fireplace is a reproduction of styles current in Britain at the time of Henry VIII. Its simple lines complement houses of many different periods. The fireback should be bare brick.

Georgian fireplace

As the eighteenth century progressed, fireplaces became less intricately embellished. The acanthus was a favorite motif, as was the Empire eagle, adopted by America as a symbol of the new republic.

English Victorian fireplace

In Victorian England, fire surrounds became simpler, and arched inserts were in vogue at the beginning of the period. As the nineteeth century progressed, rectangular grates with decorative tile inserts were added.

French fireplace

Lavish, curvy French fireplaces with their rich carving are very distinctive, dating back to the seventeenth century. Their flamboyant style has never gone out of fashion, and makes a wonderful feature in any period room.

Regency fireplace

Finely detailed Adam-style fireplaces became popular in the Federal period of the late eighteenth century, and this has long been an American favorite. The urns, garlands, and reeding are typical motifs.

Hole-in-the-wall, modern fireplace

Simple, modern hole-in-the-wall fireplaces have a pared-back elegance that looks equally striking in both refurbished period houses as well as in modern lofts.

Modern fireplace

The chimney of this gas fire runs through the center of a room. The open side provides an unusual focal point, and the glass bricks at the back offer a warm glow at the other side.

Cornices & Other Moldings

The difference even a simple cornice makes to a room can be astounding. Don't feel you have to reserve them just for high ceilings, as low ceilings that are simply squared off at the wall have the effect of seeming even lower.

Over the centuries, there have been very different styles of cornices. Although nowadays it is usually a simple rounding off, perhaps with some molding detail at the edges, in the past embellishments have ranged from the well-known egg and dart to elaborately molded cornice friezes (see opposite).

Traditionally, fibrous plasterwork was used to make the moldings, and now even small sections of these original details can be used to make a mold and so can be fully restored. All plasterwork can become clogged with layers of paint over the years. This can be scrubbed out with a brush and water, or cleaned with chemical products put on in a paste, then peeled away, removing the debris. The chemicals have to be stabilized with another solution before the plaster can be painted. It's a tricky job, but the results are astounding, revealing whole motifs that had previously disappeared under the layers of paint.

ADDING INTEREST

■ **Choose a cornice** according to the proportions of your room.

■ **Ceiling roses** generally complement the cornice design, using large motifs appropriate for a focal point. They make an elaborate setting from which to hang the beautiful chandeliers that grace period homes. Nowadays, ceiling roses have shrunk to almost nothing, as central pendants have fallen from fashion in favor of recessed spotlights and focused lighting.

■ **Corbels** are elaborate plaster brackets used as decorative features in hallways, supporting ceiling arches, or to support the mantelshelves of fireplaces.

▶ **High ideas**

This intricately molded ceiling with coordinating cornice is quite enchanting, adding grandeur to the whole interior. This one is made of plaster; in some parts of the world they are made of pressed metal.

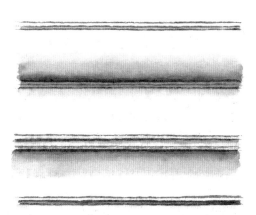

Regency fluted ceiling rose

Shaped ceiling roses with fine, low-relief designs were popular in Regency houses, as were acanthus leaves, a classic motif used throughout the Georgian and Victorian periods. Simpler ceiling roses were used in the less important rooms, such as the bedrooms (other than the master bedroom, which would have had an ornate ceiling rose).

Plain convex and concave cornices

These have a wide variety of profiles, and are now the most common styles. Convex cornices were fashionable in the 1920s and can still look very chic, retaining a clean simplicity.

Egg and dart cornice

Cornices that incorporate the egg and dart molding have retained their popularity since Georgian times.

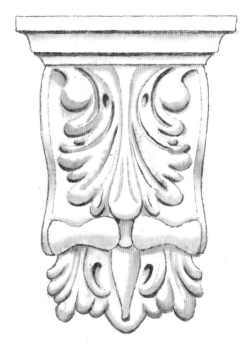

Decorative frieze cornice

The shallow relief of this elaborate cornice frieze is typical of the Regency period at the beginning of the nineteenth century.

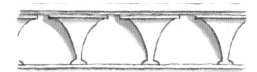

Acanthus corbel

Corbels with acanthus leaf designs were a popular style in Victorian houses.

Art Deco style cornice

These bold, fan-like motifs were popular during the Art Deco period of the 1920s.

Door & Window Furniture

Door and window furniture finishes a room in a similar way to the fastenings on a garment. The same jacket takes on quite a different look, depending on whether it has a few big, bold buttons, lines of tiny buttons, or even a discreet zipper. It's the same with interiors. Architectural ironware might not be a large element in interior design, but being metal, it attracts the light and consequently attention. Furthermore, it completes the look of the room. Whatever finish and style you choose, continue the theme throughout the house for a cohesive look.

STYLE AND FINISH

■ **First, choose a basic style:** period or modern. This need not depend on the age of your house. Period homes with updated interiors can look very good with understated modern ironware.

■ **For doors,** decide whether you want doorknobs or levers, and whether or not you want them lockable.

■ **Window furniture** is divided into fasteners that are suitable for sash windows, and those that are suitable for casements.

■ **For the finish,** a surprisingly long list is available, basically falling into the categories of black iron, brass, bronze, nickel plate, stainless steel, aluminum, chrome, anodized aluminum, color-coated, and gold-plated. In addition, most of these can then be antiqued, polished, or satin finished.

■ **Brass** is the traditional metal for ironware, but still fits well in any home and will not become out-of-date.

■ **Bronze** has a duller finish, with more of an antiqued look.

■ **The white metals,** such as chrome, nickel, and stainless steel, and color-coated ironware are more contemporary, while black iron has an old country feel to it.

■ **Reserve gold-plating** for the grandest of residences.

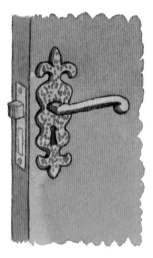

Wrought-iron lever

Black iron has an ancient look, best reserved for old rural properties; otherwise, it can look theatrical.

Georgian classic lever

The Georgian lever latch is still immensely popular. For a classic look, choose one in brass.

Antique brass oval knob

This pretty fluted oval knob in antiqued brass retains its traditional appeal.

Glass knob

Molded glass doorknobs add a delightful sparkle. They have been popular over the years.

Fancy silver handle

Beautiful sculpted chrome levers are a rare find and add individual style to any interior.

Classic chrome knob

Generally considered traditional, when made in chrome they can look chic in modern homes.

Window latches

For casement windows, you need window stays, and/or handles to open and shut them. The black iron rat-tail design above is a traditional classic, while the brass thumb-turn stay has modern appeal.

◀ Door furniture treats

The shiny quality of most door furniture introduces a gleam to the interior, and though it is a small detail, it can be seen across the room when it catches the light.

Stainless steel lever

Classy chrome makes this ideal for any modern home. It would work particularly well in houses from the Machine Age built around 1915–1939.

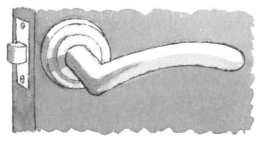

Curved modern lever

The easy action of a curved lever in satin-anodized aluminum makes this ideal for a modern family home.

Straight modern lever

The linearity of a straight bar in polished nickel such as this one has an uncompromisingly contemporary air to it.

Radiators

Traditionally, radiators were tolerated from a style point of view because the heat and comfort they gave surpassed the inconvenience of their unattractive looks. Ironically, the heavy proportions of traditional cast-iron radiators have now become much sought after. In the meantime, radiators became slimmer, but not necessarily any more beautiful, and the solution was to box them in. The drawback is that doing so inhibits the warm air flow, rendering the radiators less efficient. However, in recent years, heating engineers have woken up to the fact that radiators can be both beautiful and effective, providing interior sculpture together with warmth and comfort.

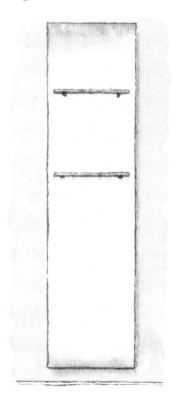

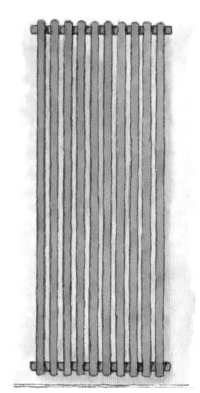

Steel flat panel

This sleek radiator can be fitted with towel racks, so it is ideal for bathrooms. Made tall, it emits plenty of heat.

Tubular column

Tubular columns can be built to any height and put together to any width. They are particularly elegant in a tall, slim configuration.

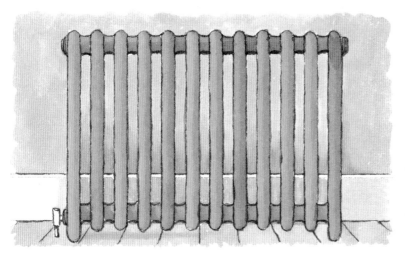

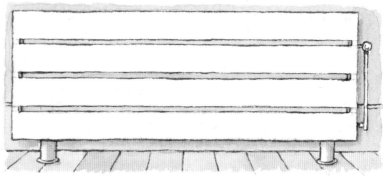

Sectional steel columns

This new version of the classic cast-iron radiator has smoothed out the lines and added color to make a feature in modern interiors. Different heights and depths of columns enable the installation of almost any width.

Horizontal flat panel

Neat horizontal panels fit well in any room, and particularly suit modern interiors. Their flat good looks conceal an efficient secret—fins that can double their heat output.

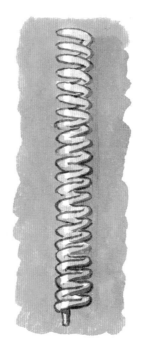

Flow form

Low, tubular radiators have a surprising heat output due to the fins incorporated in their design. Fun, modern, and available in many colors, their industrial looks would suit any contemporary apartment.

◀ Old-fashioned charm

Traditional cast-iron radiators have a sculptural quality that still holds more appeal than many of the contemporary styles. Painted white and fitted under a window, this one almost becomes part of the architecture.

Hot spring

This radiator turns heat into an art form, which deserves to be given a prominent position within the home.

EFFICIENT HEATING

■ **Each style of radiator** has a different heat output, which varies according to its surface area. Some modern double radiators look small but sandwich a series of fins between them, which greatly increases the surface area, and therefore the heat output.

■ **Choosing what is right for you** has to be undertaken in consultation with a heating engineer who will calculate the amount of heat output you need in the room and decide how large the radiators have to be.

■ **From an interior design perspective,** a radiator's aesthetics will be a consideration, and an attractive radiator could well provide the heat you need. However, if the thermal units don't add up, you may have to use a stylish yet insufficient radiator in a prominent part of the room with a workhorse that emits greater amounts of heat but is hidden in a secluded corner.

Kitchen Faucets

The days when kitchen faucets were solely high-necked pillars or a wall-mounted upright design are long gone. Now the choice is dazzling in terms of type as well as style (check out the box opposite). Bear in mind that you will need to be able to fit your pots, pans, and kettles under the tap, which, depending on the height of these, could mean you need to choose a swan neck design. If you prefer to turn on the faucets with the back of your hand, then levers are the best choice.

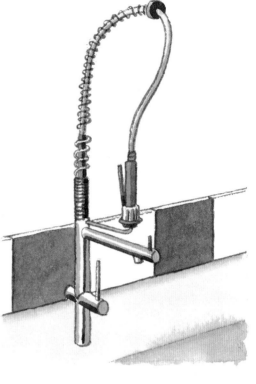

▼ Country style

The traditional styling of this shiny three-hole faucet gives it a timeless, contemporary look, perfect for any country home.

Professional kitchen faucet

The professional kitchen faucet is the twenty-first-century choice for serious cooks. It is a single-lever all-in-one unit with the controls at the spout end. A flexible hose attachment can be used to clean the worst dirt off pans and crockery, and to thoroughly rinse vegetables. Great-looking for state-of-the-art kitchens, this type of faucet needs a generous amount of water pressure to operate, so you may need to have a pump installed.

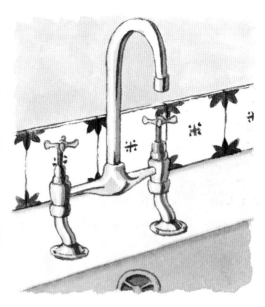

All-in-one faucet

If you want a single spout, but prefer to mix the hot and cold by hand, this elegant swan neck with handles set on the side would be right for you.

Single-lever faucet

This delightful, tall-spouted, single-lever all-in-one faucet is a practical option. You can turn the water on and off and adjust the heat with the back of your hand, keeping the lever clean, even if your hands are oily or slippery from food preparation.

Deck-mounted faucet

Bridge-pillar sink faucets have a two-hole feed, providing a simple, functional kitchen solution that has traditional resonance.

Modern single-lever faucet

Robust and modern, a single-lever all-in-one faucet adds a light, feminine touch to the kitchen sink.

Traditional bib faucets with levers

These bib faucet stands have traditional styling that has old-world appeal. The lever action means they are practical to use.

MONO AND DUAL FAUCETS

■ **For single-hole sinks,** you can choose an all-in-one faucet, either with taps or levers on either side, or with a single lever close to the spout.

■ **For dual-hole sinks,** you can have a kitchen dual-flow deck faucet, which is the modern basic standard, or a bridge-pillar sink faucet. If you want something a little more traditional in style, look to bib faucets, which are set on standpipes (see left).

■ **Within each of these categories** the styles can be remarkably different and plentiful, and what you choose for your home will be a combination of practicality, the style of your kitchen, and, of course, your personal taste.

Bathroom Faucets

Even excluding bidets and showers, the choice in bathroom faucets can be bewildering. As well as pairs of taps, you can choose bath/shower deck faucets; monoblocs, which require one hole; three-hole faucets (hot, cold, and spout); four-hole bath/shower faucets (hot, cold, shower, spout); and even five-hole bath/shower faucets (hot, cold, spout, shower, faucet). They can be wall-mounted, bath- or basin-mounted, floor-mounted (baths), or worktop-mounted (basins).

MIX AND MATCH

■ **Your choice of bathroom faucets** depends on whether you want a balanced look (a pair of taps or three-, four-, or five-hole faucet placed centrally), or an asymmetrical style (a single tap that is placed to one side).

■ **The style will also depend** on your bathroom. Period bathrooms, for example, can take the charming curves of Victorian faucets, whereas contemporary bathrooms would look good complemented by almost any style. For modern, minimalist bathrooms, you will need to look into the very latest restrained and understated designs.

Traditional three-piece basin faucet

This Victorian-style, bath-mounted bath/shower faucet is perfect for period bathrooms in either a brass or chrome finish. The same design is available wall mounted.

Single-lever faucet

This single-lever basin mixer requires only one basin hole. It can be mounted directly on the basin, or, if the basin is inset, it can be mounted on the worktop.

Traditional bath pillars

Traditional bath pillar faucets still hold much appeal for period and contemporary bathrooms. Their handles are easy to grip when hands are covered with slippery soap.

◄ Elegant curves

This swan-necked faucet looks good on a ceramic, wall-hung basin. Its simple lines perfectly complement the generous basin while leaving it uncluttered.

◄◄ Mixed media

A single-lever faucet is the elegant minimalist solution for a contemporary glass basin. These two modern materials work well together, bringing light and sparkle to the bathroom.

Surface-mounted basin faucet

A single lever on the top of this spout controls the temperature and water force. Available in tall and short styles, its minimalism would look good in a modern bathroom.

Basic basin faucet

Basic basin faucets come in many simple and elegant styles. This classic design, with separate hot and cold levers, suits both period and contemporary bathrooms.

Modern three-piece basin faucet

This elegant, minimal, three-piece basin faucet is perfect for a modern bathroom. The tall spout can be moved to one side for easy face washing.

Sinks

Your choice of fixtures dictates the style of the bathroom, and while the suite should be viewed as a whole, it is the sink styles that provide the most variety and make the largest statement; so choose these first, and then pick out a toilet and bath to match.

The choice falls into three main types: traditional pedestal, wall hung, and furniture mounted. Pedestals provide support for the basin and conceal the plumbing. Wall-hung sinks present a more modern look and come with a mounting frame that is concealed behind a false wall. The plumbing is also concealed behind a chrome bottle trap.

The third sink type is furniture mounted, and this is where there is the most variety, ranging from traditional vanity units to the very latest worktop arrangements. Although minimal in style, these have undoubtedly been influenced by traditional Victorian washbowls, with their evocative curvy basins. However, the latest square and rectangular styles are decidedly more Japanese than Victorian in their influence.

THE RIGHT STYLE

■ **Two sinks** mounted side by side can be a useful solution for modern families, relieving morning bathroom congestion. Pairs of modern worktop or wall-mounted sinks can be suitably streamlined to make this arrangement a manageable option, even in a reasonably small space.

■ **Corner sinks** can offer the best solution in space-starved bathrooms. There are many such styles available, ranging from Victorian to ultramodern.

■ **Coordinate the plumbing fixtures.** If you've chosen wall-mounted sinks, you may well opt for a cantilevered toilet, which will have a similar mounting frame to the sink, to be concealed behind a false wall along with the tank, for a sleek, modern feel.

▶ **Timeless charm**

Pedestals can incorporate any period—this generous, Edwardian-influenced sink has elegant curves that perfectly suit the unfitted style of the rest of this bathroom.

Pedestal sink

Although pedestals are a well-loved traditional style, some designs can look very modern as well. The ceramic pedestal that matches the sink provides support and conveniently neatly hides the plumbing.

Console sink

Console sinks with shapely ceramic legs have a period feel that goes particularly well with Victorian claw-footed baths. Although they are thought of as old-fashioned, their freestanding look has a modern feel.

Metal frame wall-hung sink

Wall-hung sinks need a mounting frame concealed behind a false wall. These may be further supported by a metal frame—a style that was especially popular in the early twentieth century.

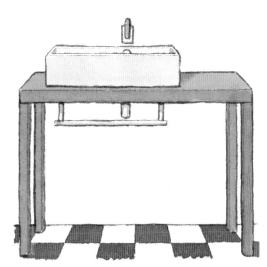

Squared-off sink

Zen-style influence has seen a proliferation of square and rectangular worktop styles. They are elegant, practical, and easy on the eye, and are often mounted on simple countertop furniture with coordinated, wheelie-drawer units that slide underneath for flexible storage.

Glass sink

Contemporary sink designs are incorporating many new materials, from glass and stainless steel to wood, stone, rubber, and vinyl. This glass sink is furniture mounted. Undersinks and wall-hung sinks in various materials are also available.

Semi-inset sink

This sink, semi-inset onto a vanity unit, has a contemporary feel and provides both storage space and a neat look. There are also sinks that can be either surface mounted or inset into vanity units, providing an even wider choice of styles.

Showers

Busy modern lifestyles mean we have less bathing time, so jumping into the shower in the morning is increasingly popular. There are three basic kinds of shower: over-bath, cubicle, and walk-in. None are particularly economical because the shower heads, valves, and faucets can be costly, and if you want a powerful jet, you're likely to need a pump, too. Site cubicles alongside baths in larger bathrooms, or give them a room of their own. Complete enclosures, combined with a shower tray, are properly waterproofed and less prone to fitting problems. You can also get enclosures that consist of two glass walls, to be used in a tiled corner of the bathroom. The most luxurious showers are the walk-in variety, offering as much space as you could need.

THE RIGHT STYLE

■ **Dual-control thermostatic valves** come in pairs: one to control the water flow, the other to control the temperature. This allows you to preset the temperature.

■ **Thermostatic temperature controls** are single dials that adjust the heat by mixing different volumes of hot and cold water. They must be used in conjunction with a shut-off valve. These control the flow of water once it has been balanced by the thermostat.

■ **Fixed shower heads** are attached to the shower wall; the pipes are concealed.

■ **Shower arms and risers** have the pipework fixed to the outside of the wall. For a traditional look, they are used in conjunction with a shower hose.

■ **Showers with riser bars** have flexible hoses that are designed to be unhooked from the bar and hand-held when in use.

■ **Shower combinations** often combine a fixed shower head with a handheld shower.

■ **Bath-shower faucets** transfer the water flow from the bath filler to an over-bath shower.

▲ **All together now**

This state-of-the-art shower room offers two fixed shower heads and one handheld shower against white mosaic tiles. The bottom three panes of the glass panel behind the shower are frosted for privacy, while letting in maximum light.

▶ **Water wall**

This magnificent painted concrete wall creates a supremely stylish and minimalist shower, furnished only with a row of shower valves, a flexible shower, and a fixed showerhead.

Window Treatments

Sleek and crisp, or soft and feminine, window treatments can dictate the whole style of a room.

▲ Soft shades

Stylish cream London shades are the ideal solution for a simple, white-painted attic room. Made of pure cream linen, they are pulled up, providing soft folds for texture and interest.

◄ Period elegance

Beautiful silken, Italian-strung drapes exude elegance, reminiscent of the fashionable Empire-line dresses of the early nineteenth century. They're the perfect choice for rooms that have tall windows.

◄◄ Light control

Sophisticated and architectural, louvered shutters are also very practical. They can be opened and closed individually to block out dazzling sunlight or to let in soft, filtered light, depending on the position of the sun, thereby providing optimal working conditions all day.

Drapes

If you love textiles—the way they hang, the way they feel, their colors, and their textures—then drapes are for you. These are the traditional window dressings that depend on a rich fullness of fabric for a stunning, finished look. The style of the drapes depends on two main considerations: the heading, and whether or not there is a pelmet or valance.

Headings influence the way the drapes are pleated, the way they hang, and their overall look. Simple pencil pleats are understated; French pleats, elegant; and goblet pleats, sumptuous.

Pelmets and valances are generally seen as more traditional, though they needn't be, depending on how elaborate they are. They can also be very useful in helping to adjust window proportions. Low windows can be made to look taller if the pelmet is set high, and narrow windows can look wider if the valance is made longer than the width of the windows.

▲ Color confidence

These beautiful pure silk drapes display a sure sense of color, demonstrated by the bold orange binding used against the deep cerise of the main fabric. Threaded onto a curtain rod, the informal gathers add to the crisp body of the fabric.

◄ Feminine charm

Wonderful, informally swagged valances with harlequin hems introduce a soft, sensuous feel to an ultrafeminine, eighteenth-century-style salon. The pale colors make it look light, airy, and surprisingly modern.

► Cream dream

Puffball headings bring softness and interest to simple, cream, full-length, pencil-pleated drapes in a classic yet contemporary living room.

On the whole, the more fabric that is used in drapes, the more luxurious they look. So, for the most sumptuous effect, have them richly gathered, lined, and interlined, then cut them long so they "puddle" onto the floor. While generously cut and beautifully made drapes may seem extravagant, traditionally they were made like this for good reason. Their thick folds provided the perfect protection against winter drafts whistling through ill-fitting windows—a major concern in the unheated houses of yesteryear. This is obviously not so much of a concern now, but there is still something very beguiling about a room dressed with lavish drapes. They offer the perfect opportunity to use beautiful textiles, enhanced by voluminous folds.

Let the drapes complement, rather than dominate, the room by bearing in mind that the windows are the light source and the drapes should echo that. The most successful fabric choices are those that are lighter than, or the same tone as, the walls.

WHAT'S IN A HEADING?

■ **Pencil pleats** are the perfect choice for curtains that are complemented by a valance or a pelmet board. The fabric requirement is twice the length of the curtain rod.

■ **French or pinch pleats** form an stylish, deep heading that looks good on longer curtains hung on a curtain rod. The fabric requirement is at least two-and-a-half times the length of the curtain rod.

■ **Goblet pleats** are a more relaxed, feminine version of French pleats with gathered, rather than pleated, sections. The fabric requirement is two-and-a-half times the length of the curtain rod.

■ **A puffball** is a witty heading created by adding a fold of fabric at the drape top, which, when gathered, results in a frothy puffball. The fabric requirement is twice the length of the curtain rod.

■ **Diamond smocking,** using transfer dots, is a pretty, hand-sewn heading. It looks best where the detail can be seen. The fabric requirement is twice the length of the curtain rod.

◀ Empire style
Graceful swags and tails date back to the early nineteenth century. These, in sensuous golden silk, make a sophisticated window treatment.

◀◀ Fixed pelmet
An elegant fixed pelmet, painted cream and decorated with Adam-style motifs, successfully sets off simple gathered curtains.

Tieback style
Tiebacks can be made as informal ties, like this, for a casual look, or buckram-backed for a more formal style.

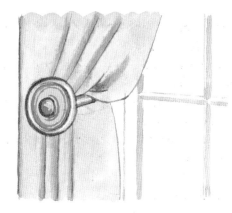

Holdbacks
Holdbacks, most of which are made from wood, metal, or porcelain, are usually sold alongside coordinating curtain rods.

127

Swags and tails
This elaborate style looks best on larger windows. The wider the window, the more swags you can include.

Valances
To improve window proportions, adjust them with a valance, a fixed structure made of wood, which surrounds the window.

Panels & Modern Curtains

While traditional drapes depend on the lavish use of fabric, with modern panels and curtains, the opposite is true. If minimalism is your style, gathers are a no-no, because contemporary window treatments are designed to enhance rather than shroud the architecture. Drapes have gradually shrunk to panels, bringing with them a refreshing light and airy look.

Quite apart from the fashion element of this about-face, one of the reasons for these more minimal window treatments is that, with centrally heated homes, we are now able to dispense with draft-excluding drapes. Gathered and pleated headings have given way to tab- or tie-tops, hooks, clips, and rings. Traditional rods and valances have disappeared, and in their place are fine metal or wooden rods, tension wires, and hooks. Finials in metal, glass, or porcelain trim the ends of rods like jewels.

▲ Sweet solution

Tab-topped curtains look pretty hung on rods painted white. For softness in the bedroom, buy the drapes slightly too wide for the window so they fall into gentle folds once in position.

◀ Translucent style

White translucent panels dress a pair of French doors to continue the tone of the walls to make a fresh background for a colorful modern interior.

◀◀ All tied up

Instead of the usual holdbacks, use a pretty satin ribbon to tie up the middle of ultrafeminine lace panels and let in the morning light.

WHICH TOPPING?

■ **When using curtain clips,** check their weight-bearing capacity to ensure they'll be able to hold the fabric.

■ **Unusual curtain rings** can be found in all sorts of places. Shackles from yachting chandlers, for example, can make excellent rings for hanging up panels.

■ **Ribbons** make delightful, feminine ties for bedroom panels. Or use strips of the same fabric as the panel itself, stitched or buttoned onto the material.

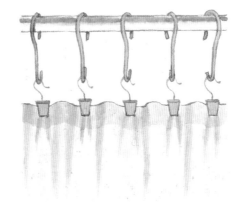

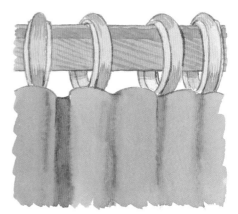

Straight laced

Lacy panels are so pretty, they're best seen flat so the design can be most appreciated. Many come with scalloped hems.

All hooked up

The combination of curtain clips and hooks makes a feature of a simple hanging system for a translucent panel.

Painted rings

Beautiful old painted curtain rings can become a feature of simple modern window treatments. Hook onto ungathered drapes.

Panels can either be bought ready-made—with tab- or tie-tops for hanging on rods, or plain-topped for use with curtain clips; or you can easily make your own. As well as looking at upholstery fabric, search for suitable materials in dress fabric departments, antique shops (old linens make wonderful panels), and Asian markets, where you can find beautiful silks. Just cut the fabric to size and hem it, then clip the panels into position. Add interesting trims using braid, binding, fringing, or bobbles, or bring individual style by stitching on feathers (from craft, haberdashery, or fishing shops), tiny shells (buy them predrilled from craft shops), buttons, or bells.

The simplicity of panels suits modern and period houses alike, but works best on windows of good proportion. Without the help of valances and pelmets, there's little a panel can do to enhance inappropriate window dimensions.

◀ Dream topping

A garland of fake flowers gently swagged across the top of the window adds a feminine touch to a simple panel.

◀◀ Period style

Although ultimately modern, panels can be used to enhance period windows. Here, just three brass bosses are used to hang up and hold back a sheer white organdie panel, which adds a tailored yet ethereal look to the dining room.

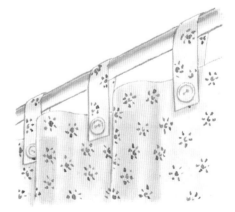

Eyelets and tension wires

Use tension wires in conjunction with curtain clips or with an eyelet heading, which can be made using DIY eyelets.

Simple ties

Ties make an attractive, modern heading. Cut them wide, as here, or narrow, and then tie into position on a curtain rod.

Buttoned tabs

Add interest to an ordinary tab heading by sewing on some beautiful buttons. Choose bold ones to be seen from a distance.

Soft Shades

Pretty yet sophisticated, soft shades have a timeless charm that suits all styles of architecture. Ranging from ultrafeminine Austrian to Roman, there's a design to suit every taste; yet they never shroud the architecture, which gives them a modern edge. Austrian shades can have a gathered heading, and they gather vertically, too, as they pull up, but most other types of shade remain flat, giving a clean, tailored look.

Plain fabrics work well on all shades, as do vertical stripes and striped ethnic fabrics, such as ikats, but make sure there is enough width in the shade to incorporate a satisfactory number of repeats. Patterned fabrics can present more of a problem, because you will need to work out what it will look like when the shade is pulled up. It is worth finding a solution, though, because shades do not use excessive amounts of fabric and, being flat, show off fabrics at their best.

132

▲ All white
The zigzag bottom edge and translucent fabric of these Roman shades add up to an elegant window treatment. Custom-made to fit each window, they are also a good way to deal with the curve of a bay.

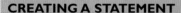

CREATING A STATEMENT

■ **Shades are the ideal companion** to elaborate fixed drapes, as the curtains can be left undisturbed and the shades pulled down to shut out the night.

■ **Bold motifs** look wonderful on larger shades. They need to be positioned carefully, so allow for extra fabric.

■ **Add bottom-edge trims** for interest to flat shades that pull up from the top, such as roller or Roman.

■ **Side and top trims** work well on shades that roll or pull up from the bottom, such as Swedish, tied, and London shades.

■ **Fabrics with integral borders** can be adapted to suit your shade. Simply trim off the borders and reposition them where you want them on the made-up shade.

■ **Add a pretty touch** to sheer shades by using ribbons instead of cords for pulling up. They'll show through to the front of the translucent fabric at the same time as bringing interest to the back.

Roman classic

The most useful shade of all, Romans can be used on their own or in conjunction with drapes for flexible light control.

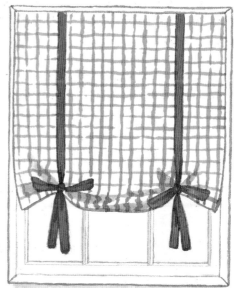

◄ **Sweet as candy**

Candy-striped pull-up shades are pretty in pink. It's a delightfully feminine look that's emphasized by gorgeous, girly rosette tie-ups.

▲ **Linen and lace**

Blue check household linen can be made into Roman shades. The deep lace edging adds a decorative touch.

All tied up

This attractive variation on the Swedish theme is simply rolled up and tied in position with colorful ribbons.

Architectural Shades

Stylish and modern, structured shades have an architectural feel. Far more engineered than any other window treatment, they are usually made to order and many have a sophisticated mechanism for controlling light. Ranging from the classic Venetian to sleek, pleated conservatory shades—which are individually designed to fit each windowpane, whatever its shape—there is a style of shade to suit each situation. Some can be made to pull up from the windowsill, which are useful for rooms such as ground-floor offices, where plenty of natural light is needed for working, yet there is a need for street level privacy.

MAKING YOUR CHOICE

■ **Translucent Japanese paper shades** supported by horizontal bamboo strips are a delightful light-filtering alternative to split cane.

■ **Venetian shades** have wooden or lightweight aluminum slats, which are made in various widths; some are even perforated.

■ **Dim-out shades** are useful if you want to cut out lots of light. They come in white and colors as well as the more usual black.

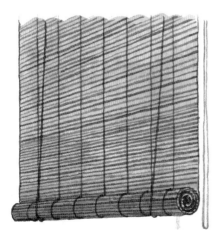

Split cane simplicity
Inexpensive and surprisingly sophisticated, split cane shades have a natural, neutral quality that will never be dated.

Vertical option
Give a cool, modern look to the home office with a vertical shade. The slats can be pivoted to cut out glare at all times of the day.

▲ **Over the top**
Clever conservatory blinds can be individually made to virtually any size or shape. These ones provide an imaginative solution for a modern bathroom extension.

▶ **Pleats, please**
A wall of windows and doors that look out onto the swimming pool are fitted with pleated blinds that are raised and lowered individually for the ultimate in light control. With the shades fitted directly onto the frames, the doors can be opened and closed whether the shades are up or down.

Shutters

An integral part of the architecture, shutters need to be custom-made to fit the windows. Traditionally constructed of wood, they were originally designed to deal with the local climate. As a result, Georgian houses in chilly regions on either side of the Atlantic majored in paneled shutters. The shutters folded neatly into shallow recesses on either side of the windows, ready to be closed against cold winter nights. In the sunny Caribbean, meanwhile, louvered plantation shutters had quite a different function. Normally kept closed during the day, they protected the interior from the dazzle and heat of the noonday sun. The louvers could be adjusted throughout the day so the light could gently filter through to the room.

Along with many things minimal, shutters are undergoing a revival; they're a favorite with architects and designers because they enhance, rather than shrouding, elegant windows. They can be hinged into position or set on runners in front of the windows as sliding screens. There's also a far wider choice than ever of materials available for making shutters, such as sandblasted glass, polypropylene, and metal mesh.

PANELS AND LOUVERS

■ **Paneled shutters** are a classic design, and are made as a single shutter per window, or in top and bottom sections, that can be opened and closed independently.

■ **Plantation shutters** are made up of wooden louvers that are opened and closed using a central strut. They can be made as single panels, or divided into top and bottom sections, cowboy saloon style, for flexibility.

■ **Fancy paneled shutters** can have sandblasted glass panels to provide privacy rather than to control the light, modern metal mesh, or carved fretwork made from medium-density fiberboard.

▶ **Shaped to measure**
Being made to measure, shutters can come in any shape to suit the architecture. These Gothic-style pointed-top shutters perfectly complement the steeply angled eaves of their surroundings.

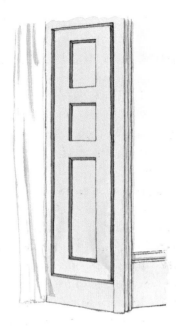

Neat solution

Classic Georgian paneled shutters were craftily designed to fit into recesses built within the window reveals.

Light sensitive

Adjust louvered plantation shutters to filter the light or to shut it out altogether. As the sun goes down, throw them wide open.

Soft Furnishings

Upholstery and cushions, bolsters and throws: these are the ingredients of home style and comfort.

▲ Sofa comfort

Tightly covered sofas bring both comfort and style to the living room. Matching bolsters add coordinated ease—throw in extra scatter cushions for luxury.

◄ Color flair

Asian silks are made in a rainbow of shades, adding zest to the interior. Cushions need very little fabric, so you can splash out on a range of coordinating or complementary hues. Use them all together, as here, or change them to suit the seasons.

◄◄ Cushion style

Buttons and tassels, embroidery and appliqué—these are just some of the ways you can add interest to cushions.

Sofas & Chairs

Sinking into a sumptuous sofa at the end of the day is what coming home is all about—total relaxation and a sense of well-being within your surroundings. Upholstery is not an item you'll want to buy on a regular basis, so for it to last you need to choose enduring style as well as comfort.

You may soon tire of a hasty buy chosen purely on the basis of current esthetics, so try to visualize your needs, certainly over the next five years. If you have young children and love cream décor, close-covered sofas may not be the best choice, but if those covers are removable and washable, there's no reason why you should compromise your style for something simply because "it doesn't show stains."

▶ Loose comfort

Cottagey sofas covered in antique duck egg blue linen look inviting. The comfort factor is enhanced by the overly large cushions covered in a strikingly different color.

▼ Sleek and modern

Simple, straight lines with low back and arms, this style emanates from pure sixties chic, and is enjoying a revival in the twenty-first century. While this style is elegant, check to see that the seat is deep enough to make up for the low back.

When it comes to quality, you need both to try the furniture for comfort and to check the construction. Good upholstery is timber or steel framed with interior-sprung seating, which is then wrapped in a high-density foam. The whole piece is finally cushioned with a padding made of a material such as cotton or polydacron to protect both the timber frame and the calico upholstery cover.

Decorative upholstery covers are either tailored to fit or made loose and removable for cleaning.

▲ **Twin bonus**
Matching chairs with no arms offer versatile seating. Set them side by side to make a sofa or use them singly, depending on how many people you need to seat.

▲ Smooth lines

The sensuous curved back of this sofa transforms what could be a functional piece into one that perfectly suits its elegant period surroundings.

◄ Side chair style

While sofas can provide the bulk of comfortable seating, side chairs can add great flair and style. Look for interesting shapes, such as this long-legged chair with curvy arms.

CHOOSING YOUR SOFA

■ **Sofa styles** are broadly influenced by either the high-backed Victorian wingbacks or the well-known and loved Chesterfield, (named after the nineteenth-century English earl), with back and arms the same height.

■ **Comfort** depends on the right relationship between the back and arm height and the depth of the seat. Try before you buy, making sure you take up a comfortable "television watching position." Depending on how tall you are, whatever the sofa looks like, it may simply not suit you.

■ **Corner sofas** are very useful. They're the ideal choice where space is tight, for a modern look that also provides plenty of seating.

Cushions & Throws

Fresh cushions and throws are a quick and inexpensive way of reviving an interior that is looking tired. Give classic sofas a decidedly fashionable edge with the addition of accessories in the latest colors and styles. You need only short lengths of fabric and trims, so you can afford to buy exotic textiles and take advantage of remnants to make up the most interesting cushions and throws.

Cushion pads are available inexpensively, either synthetic or feather-filled, and in all shapes and sizes: square, oblong, round, and bolster. Feathers plump up in a beautifully squashy, sumptuous way, but if you are an allergy sufferer, synthetic would be a better option.

There is a huge choice of throws available to buy, too. Choose them for color or pattern to bring added interest to the upholstery, and customize them, if you like, by adding fringes, beading, or bobbles for extra personality. Casually draped over the arm or back of a sofa, or at the end of your bed, throws will make your living room and bedroom look even more stylish.

BUTTONS AND BOWS

■ **Piping** adds a crisp finish. Use it in contrast to the body of the cushion for a city-smart feel.

■ **Fringes and bobble trims** introduce a fun, flirty feel. Choose restrained colors for a traditional look, bold contrasts for modern style.

■ **Buttons** add interest to cushions in the same way they do to clothes. Use them big and bold for a confident statement, or line up tiny pearl buttons for a pretty, feminine finish.

■ **Size matters.** Big, squashy cushions have a sumptuous, relaxed feel; little ones add a decorative, perky touch. Use several different sizes for a "layered" look.

■ **Use cushions for introducing accent colors** to the interior. An elegantly tonal scheme can be given seasonal zest with the introduction of a touch of contrast.

▲ **Patchwork pieces**
Add color using patchwork. Make up some classic American styles for a pretty country feel, or use large pieces, such as these, for a cleaner, more contemporary look.

▶ **Throws of color**
Use throws to add color through the seasons. This golden throw brings a touch of the fall to a cool, minimalist bedroom. At the end of the winter, spring green—mimicking the leaves of bulbs—would brighten the room once the days start to lengthen again.

Lighting

*Clever lighting is the key to creating ambience—
aim to change the mood at the flick of a switch.*

▲ On the wall

This candle wall sconce has been used to highlight a beautiful fireplace, and was added after the interior decoration was completed. Electrified wall sconces should be planned before the decoration, as the cables need to be built into the walls.

◀ Getting theatrical

Ceiling-mounted halogen track lights have more than a hint of the theatrical about them. These fittings are not designed to be discreet, but to add to the interior design of the whole room—and in a practical way, too.

◀◀ Hanging sculptures

Translucent paper stretched over wire frames have here been fastened together to create huge pendants. Grouped together like this, they make the most dramatic of centerpieces for a stairwell.

Planning Ahead

Flexibility is the key to good lighting because within one design you'll need to incorporate general, task (for reading, cooking, and working), and mood lighting. Planning for all this can be daunting for most of us, so it's tempting to leave the lighting until last, when everything else is in its place. This is a mistake. If you can visualize where furniture will go, and how you would like the room to look, make planning the lighting one of your first priorities. In that way, the wiring can be chased into the walls or pulled through to ceiling positions at an early stage, before the decorators arrive.

Start with the general lighting. A modern, flexible, and subtle solution is to use several downlights recessed into the ceiling, or surface-mounted spotlights. These may all be wired to the same switch, or, depending on the size of the room, you may "zone" them, wiring groups of individual lights to different switches. The lights in different parts of the room can then be switched on and off to alter the mood or focus. The number of lights you need for each area depends on what the room will be used for and the amount of light each fixture emits. In the hall and stairway, for example, you'll need to plan for plenty of light for safety, while living room lighting can be more subdued.

Next, tackle task lighting. Reading, writing, and any kind of close work requires excellent light levels. Classic work lamps are still very efficient and stylish, or you may prefer to use spotlights, either as table or standard lamps. Kitchen work surfaces need a different kind of light again. Many kitchen suppliers fit fluorescent lights under wall cupboards to shine down on countertops. Alternatively, you could fit two, three, or more ceiling-hung lamps with reflective metal shades, ceiling-mounted spotlights, or closely spaced downlights. Finally, go for drama. Narrow-beam spotlights produce a very intense light, which can be used to create special effects, focusing, for example, on an interesting architectural feature in the room, or a piece of sculpture.

▶ **Variable lighting**
Neat, recessed downlights, spaced at regular intervals throughout this kitchen-diner, provide plenty of general light for the whole space. The lights are switched on and off in groups so, for example, the kitchen lights can be switched off while you dine. Six pendant spots over the counters add efficient task lighting exactly where it's needed.

Recessed spotlights

Use recessed downlights with regular or wide-angle beams in groups. They need to be fitted into the ceiling void. Many are low voltage and work in conjunction with a transformer. Ask your electrician how many you will need. They come in standard voltage, too. Standard-voltage lamps do not usually give out as much light at low voltage, and they can need replacing more often.

Triple ceiling spots

Grouped spotlights, such as this triple set, can be surface mounted and directed outward to offer efficient general lighting.

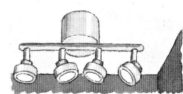

Quad ceiling track and spots

Spotlights on a track use only one electrical outlet, yet allow several sources of directional light aimed at focal points or dark corners.

Recessed eyeball spotlight

Downlights come as standard fixed, or as eyeball, which means the light can be directed to bounce off a wall, for example.

Low-voltage wire spotlights

Wire spotlight systems are an attractive, modern, lightweight solution that can be surface mounted and so require no making good or redecorating after fitting. They can also be used to span areas such as voids under roof lights.

Single glass spot

Single spotlights, such as this glass cube one, are perfect for creating dramatic effects. Fit them with a narrow-beam halogen lamp to create an intense light, good for highlighting.

Pendants & Wall Lights

In the days before electric light, beautiful central chandeliers and candle wall sconces were the only lighting options. They weren't overly efficient in terms of the light emitted, but the mood they created has never been surpassed. With the introduction of electric light, these fittings were simply replaced with electrified versions of the same fittings, but tungsten bulbs (see opposite) in strong enough wattages to produce enough overall light resulted in a stark ambience.

However, those traditional lights themselves were almost sculptural in their beauty, providing interest high in the room, and we still love the look of central and wall lights fitted with bulbs of a more subtle wattage when they are supplementing other means of general lighting.

Most rooms have central ceiling roses, so there's little worry about early planning for pendants. However, decorative wall sconces do need to be planned early on, as the wires have to be built into the wall before decorating begins.

▲ Triple treat

A trio of blown-glass pendant lamps, hung over a modern table, add mood lighting for extra ambience when dining. Introducing the only splash of color in an otherwise black and white room, they are also a focal point in the area at all times of the day.

◀ Reflected glory

A magnificent chandelier deserves showing off, and this one has been hung above a dining table for just that reason. The mirror leaning against the wall behind means the whole ensemble is reflected, giving double exposure to the fine lighting.

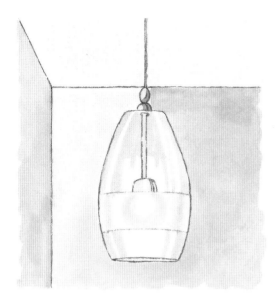

Frosted glass pendant

Single glass pendants look fresh, chic, and modern. The frosted glass band on this one cuts bulb glare, yet retains a translucent quality. Use it as a feature on its own, or hang several in a line for greater impact.

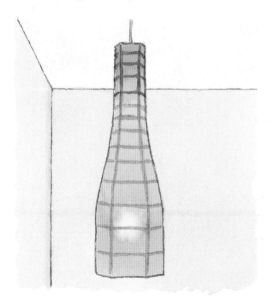

Paper pendant

Paper-shade pendants are inexpensive and come in many interesting shapes and sizes. They're the perfect quick-fix solution for any living area or bedroom.

Metal pendant

Metal-shade pendants direct the light downward and have a workmanlike quality. They're great as task lighting in workrooms or hung in lines above a kitchen countertop.

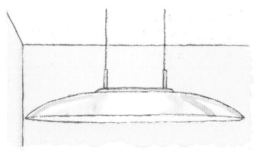

Flat frosted pendant

Flat halogen pendants provide sophisticated and efficient lighting. They are ideal for hanging over desks, work areas, or even dining tables.

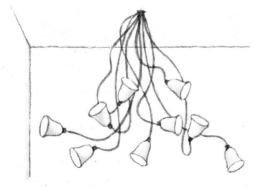

Steel twist multipendant

A steel twist multipendant is a whimsical lamp that can make a statement hanging over a dining table.

LAMPS (BULBS)

■ **Although most people** call the light source a bulb, this is a misnomer. In the professional lighting world, the bulb is called a "lamp," and this encompasses fluorescent tubes, spots, and old-fashioned "bulbs."

■ **Tungsten** or incandescent lamps are the standard domestic filament lamp. They come in various wattages, and emit a warm light. Use metal shades to direct the light emitted by spotlights, which can be further enhanced if the lamps are internally silvered or crown (top) silvered.

■ **Halogen lamps** are actually a combination of a tungsten filament with halogen gas, which gives out a brighter, whiter light than standard lamps.

■ **Low-voltage halogen lamps** are tiny compared with standard-sized lamps. Operating on 12 volts, they have to be used in conjunction with a transformer. Low-voltage fittings can be downlights, spotlights, table, or standard lamps. Individual lamps often have an integral transformer, but for downlights, the transformer comes separately, and each one may run several downlights.

■ **Fluorescent tubes** are often used in kitchens under wall cupboards to light work surfaces, and in bathrooms to create adequate light for shaving and make up. The tubes are cheap and efficient to run, yet emit plenty of clear light. They come in a series of colors, which affect the kind of light they put out. Ask for tubes that emit a light that is closest to daylight.

151

Decorative Lights

Decorative lighting is as much about the looks of the fittings as the light they emit. Many lamps introduce an almost sculptural element to a room, even during the day when they are not used. At night, when they are switched on, they provide pleasing pools of light in key areas, lending drama or accentuating focal points.

Most decorative lamps are plugged into wall sockets, so choosing these fittings often can be left until after the room is completed. The sockets may be wired to switches near the door so the lamps can be used for general lighting in rooms that rely on lighting more for ambience than for tasks.

Whatever form of lighting you choose, you can install dimmer switches. These not only provide instant mood change, but also help to prolong bulb life, both because they use less electricity when they are their dimmest and because the light is turned on gradually, rather than "jolted" on.

▶ **Double standards**
A decorative pair of standard lamps draw the eye to a charming chaise longue, while also adding extra light in the evenings for reading.

Ceramic-base table lamp
Ceramic table lamps come custom-made in a wide range of sizes and can be very tall and elegant, giving decorative impact to a room, especially when used in pairs.

Art Nouveau table lamp
Pretty Tiffany lamps with their molded glass shades were popular in the early twentieth century, but their light, feminine, sculptural look has ensured them enduring popularity.

Small oval table lamp
Contemporary table lamps that reflect traditional shapes, such as this one, can be made of different materials, such as perspex, chrome, or glass.

TASK LIGHTING

■ **Reading, writing,** and any kind of close work requires excellent light levels. Classic work lamps are efficient and stylish, or you may prefer to use spotlights as table or standard lamps.

■ **Kitchen work surfaces** need a different kind of light. Many suppliers fit fluorescent lights under wall cupboards to shine on work surfaces. Alternatively, you could fit two, three, or more ceiling-hung lamps with reflective metal shades, ceiling-mounted spotlights, or downlights.

■ **Narrow-beam spotlights** produce a very intense light, which can be used to create special effects—focusing, for example, on an interesting architectural feature in the room or a piece of sculpture.

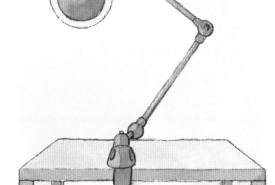

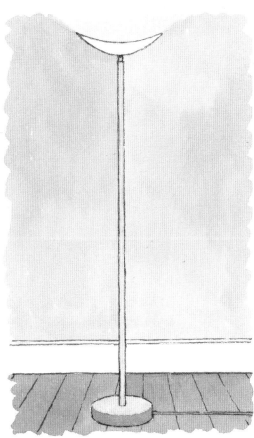

Jielde work lamp
Classic work lamps have an engineered quality that has proved timeless. This Jielde work lamp dates back to the Machine Age of the early twentieth century, and still looks handsome.

Floor uplighter
Uplighters bounce light off the ceiling, providing a soft, reflected light. This floor-standing halogen uplight gives out a clear white light. Many also feature an additional arm fitted with a spotlight.

French standard lamp
French standard lamps have an unfussy, almost workmanlike, quality that has timeless appeal. The same classic design, but scaled down, is available as table lamps.

Pictures & Displays

Express yourself with the art you hang on the wall and the objects you choose to display.

▲ Perfect arrangement

This striking cow's head print has been used as a focal point for a variety of objects arranged on the table. Everything is linked by colors picked out of the print, thereby creating a cohesive montage.

◄ Regular order

Sailing ships, identically mounted and framed, and hung close together in rows to cover a whole wall, make a striking background. The fact that the prints are traditional matters not a bit in this modern apartment, because the white frames match the style of the room.

◄◄ All together

Fine black frames give a sense of unity to pictures of disparate sizes. The smallest have been grouped to suggest a single item, giving them emphasis. The brightly painted wall sets off the whole arrangement.

Pictures

The art we choose to display on our walls is the ultimate in self-expression. It doesn't have to be collectable art: there are some wonderful prints and posters around that can be picked up inexpensively, or you may like to produce some art yourself. Canvases, abstractly painted in wonderful colors—even with latex paint—can look good, especially if used to emphasize your color scheme. Children, too, can produce some wonderful pieces with paints, crayons, or even photography, which can quickly become treasured possessions. Whatever art you choose, the skill of display comes with your choice of mount and frame, and the way you arrange them on the wall.

HANG-UPS

■ **Generous mounts** always enhance artworks, giving them room to breathe. Double mounts impart a sense of importance.

■ **Flat frames** have a modern style; elaborate profiles tend to look more traditional.

■ **Hang pictures** to relate to furniture or architectural features. Take into consideration how you will most often see them in the room. In a living room, for example, hang a painting in relation to the sofa, as it will be viewed from the sitting position.

■ **Make a statement,** either by hanging one very special large piece, or by grouping smaller pictures together.

▲▶ To order
Similar prints in identical frames, hung in ordered rows, are seen as one large piece, giving impact to the whole group.

▶ Going up
The side of a stairway is often "dead" space. Here it is put to good use with prints in delicate gilt frames, hung as a group going up the stairs.

▶▶ Mirror image
By cladding the wall with a mirror and hanging an eclectic collection, a feature has been made both of the view and the pictures.

Displays

It is the personal touches that transform a house into a home. The collected, the inherited, and the gift-given things of sentimental value provide a snapshot of memories all around us. Display them with impact so they can be appreciated at their best.

Large items easily make a statement with their size, shape, and possibly their colors. Smaller things are a little more tricky, but they can be intriguing simply because of their size. If you want to make a greater impact, gather them together into grouped displays on shelves, in glass cupboards, or in box frames hung on the walls.

▼ Contrast solution

This huge, striking vase has been given a place of honor on a stair windowsill. A single item, it makes an excellent display piece, not just because of its size—in bright lemon yellow, it adds a dramatic splash of color to a black and white stairwell.

ORGANIZATION

■ **Color** provides a link between disparate items. For example, china, glass, linen, and even tinware in classic blue and white can look surprisingly dramatic when grouped for display. Cream, too, works well as a linking color, even if your possessions are a combination of antique and modern.

■ **Make a focal point** of large, bold items by setting them on display in a prominent position. This works particularly well if you use contrasting colors.

■ **Give importance** to small items by grouping them by kind. For example, you may have a collection of hearts or cupids, beadwork, or tiny hand-painted thimbles, which would be lost on their own but look good when grouped together.

■ **Use containers for collections** of small items. Glass jars are particularly useful, as items can be viewed through them. Pretty shells or painted eggs look stunning displayed in this way. Group several jars to create even more impact.

■ **Cubby holes** or a series of shelves can also be useful for display, making a domestic gallery for your favorite things.

◀ **Make an exhibition**
Objects of all kinds look good displayed on shelves designed specially to suit them. These shelves are the correct height for each piece, and have also been divided vertically so everything has a suitable space. Making "cubby holes" like these gives the collection a museum-like sense of importance.

Room
by Room

Halls, Corridors & Stairs

Make a memorable welcome by asserting your great style on the main artery that links all the floors and rooms of the house.

◀◀◀ White idea

Pure white is the most light-reflective "color"—an excellent choice for narrow halls that are often lacking in natural light. Here, the white has been given a sharp designer edge with contrasting black "trims" on the handrail, stair treads, and diamond-spotted floor.

◀◀ Fair square

Open, square halls are an asset. They're more often blessed with windows (and therefore natural light) than their long, narrow cousins, and, as they have space for congregating in, they are immediately welcoming.

◀ High light

Natural wood window frames are complemented by cream paint along this upper-floor corridor. With plenty of windows, it is bathed in daylight. If the architecture of a house does not allow for a whole corridor of windows, such as here, the fitting of a skylight can make a huge difference, not only to the upper corridors but also to those lower down in the house, as light floods down the stairwell.

◀◀◀ Gallery space

Corridors offer great gallery space. Place sculptures as focal points at the end of those that are long and narrow; hang artwork on walls to add personality. The confined space means both can be fully appreciated close up.

Making a Welcome

Halls, corridors, and stairways comprise the main artery of the house, reflecting and affecting the overall look and feel of the home. More than simply making an impression on visitors, this area can alter your whole sense of well-being. Moving from one well-decorated room to another through a neglected hall can be depressing indeed. There are several particular considerations when planning the decoration of these areas.

Consider the light: Light is welcoming. Whether you're stepping in from a bright sunny day or a chilly, dark night, you don't want to be greeted by gloom. Nor do you want to pass from sunny living areas into the darkness of the center of the house. Good light is also always a wise safety precaution. Narrow halls are quickly "littered" by even a couple of bags and discarded shoes, and stairways have to be negotiated while carrying the

▶ Living hall

If you have the luxury of a hall that's more baronial than suburban, turn it into a welcoming living area, furnishing the middle and allowing plenty of circulation space around the edges.

▼ Lime light

Halls can take strong color because you move through the space, rather than relaxing in it. Lime might seem an irritating color, but it's a good one for a hall, as it reflects plenty of light and goes well with many other hues.

▼◀ Architectural statement

This striking staircase makes a strong architectural statement running through the house. The natural wood colors are picked up by the tiled floor and sandy colors of the wallpaper.

paraphernalia of life—both hazards indeed, and not to be attempted in the half light.

Start by considering the light you have and making the most of it. If there are no windows opening into the space, consider putting glass panels into some of the doors, to make use of "borrowed" light from outer rooms. Hang large, decorative mirrors to reflect, and therefore maximize, any natural light. For background lighting, low-voltage recessed spotlights are discreet and can emit plenty of light. Decorative pendants and wall lights put out less, but can offer extra light where it's needed.

Decoration decisions: The hall, corridor, and stairs provide the main link that runs through the house, opening out into very different styles of room, so you need a strong decorative statement that lends style to the whole house. You can afford to be adventurous because these are areas you travel through, rather than spend time relaxing in. Choose colors that will complement all the colors in the house to create harmonious vistas.

Make it hardwearing: These areas are often narrow, and so take plenty of knocks. If you are painting your walls, choose a washable paint. On the floor, the hall takes the lion's share of dirt from the street; this is dealt with best by stone, ceramic, or wood, all of which provide efficient washdown surfaces. A large coir entrance mat, fitted hall-width (preferably into a well, so the top is level with the main floor), is an excellent idea, as it takes up the worst of the incoming soil, protecting the rest of the floor against damage caused by grit.

Hide the clutter: Coats aren't gorgeous, so find a place to hide them away. Under the stairs might sound obvious—but that's because it works. If you don't have an under-the-stairs area, fix up some hooks around a corner and out of sight, or, better still, if you have the space, have a small cupboard built.

Think slim: Whether you're furnishing halls or corridors, think slim. Console tables are narrow for a reason: you need somewhere to put the mail and keys, but generous space is not a virtue of many halls. Likewise, for landings and corridors, search out pretty narrow tables, chests, and chairs; or tall, striking, floor-standing pots or bundles of sticks to add drama.

▶ **Filtering light**
With light flooding down the stairwell, through the window on the left and from the end of the corridor, this interesting hallway is spared from the lack of light that blights many other such areas.

Staircases

Running like a huge sculpture through the house, the staircase is the main architectural feature in most interiors. We're not always aware of this, because many are blocked and hidden away—often due to building safety regulations. Although there's little that can be done about that, the three-dimensional quality of staircases can still be made into a feature. For example, you can use striking flooring and wall décor on the stairwell to make a bold feature that runs vertically through the house.

The otherwise unused space of stairways is also a great opportunity for making focal points as you go up or down the stairs. Stand unusual pieces of furniture or sculpture on landings and hang favorite paintings—there's always space here for grouping them *en masse*—that can be enjoyed close-up.

▲ Elegant simplicity

Open-tread stairs allow for optimum natural light. Here, they have been complemented by minimal decoration—the most eye-catching being the wall of wooden cupboards embellished only by a line of handles.

◄ Precision pictures

When it comes to pictures, position is everything on stairways. These fish prints have been grouped together for maximum impact, then placed in the perfect position to be appreciated from all levels.

► Bold contrast

These white-tiled stairs have black borders, designed to make a strong modern statement that sets the theme for the whole stairway. It has been decorated completely in white, with black accessories for added interest.

TAKE ONE ROOM:
Sunny Hallway

The joyous yellow and green color scheme of this hall makes a wonderful background for a magnificent, eclectic collection of pictures, furniture, lamps, vases, and pots. The strong shades hold everything together and make a feature of the calculated clutter that gives this hall its personality. The pictures, in assorted sizes, are unified by the same style of frame. This is further emphasized by arranging them in neat rows with their bottom edges aligned.

The beautiful Turkish runner, with its distinctive geometric pattern, perfectly complements this bright and busy hall. The oriental design is timeless. Originally made by and for nomadic tribes, it is also very hardwearing, and when it comes to cleaning, it can be taken up, hung on a line and beaten clean with a traditional carpet beater.

A bold color scheme makes a strong statement throughout the house, while bringing cohesion to a cluttered style.

REFERENCE POINT

■ Displaying pictures to best effect is an art form in its own right. See pages 154–157 for some hints and tips.

■ The choice of rug styles is wide. To help inform your decision, see pages 88–89.

■ Get your color right in the hallway and you will immediately make a warm and welcoming impression. The art of color on pages 32–35 gives advice.

Hallways can make the best of gallery spaces. Strong, demanding paintings don't fight with the need for a relaxed ambience as they may in living rooms, for example, and they can be hung side-by-side all along the walls.

Strong color statements work well in hallways, especially when carried along all the corridors, stairways, and landings, providing a link that runs through the house. This yellow hallway has been given a green accent color on the woodwork to add personality.

Decorative lighting brings interest to a hallway, but should not be relied upon to provide enough background lighting for this potentially hazardous area. Either add wall sconces along the length of the hall or corridor, several pendants, or a row of spotlights attached to, or recessed into, the ceiling.

Slimline furniture such as console tables, narrow chests, or chairs in proportion to the long, narrow space, are the best hallway solution. This is also important from a safety aspect, as there should always be free access to all exits from the house in case of fire.

Runners make an excellent hallway flooring solution. This beautiful handwoven rug has classic red and indigo tones that have timeless appeal. Oriental rugs are hardwearing, and, being patterned, tolerant of the occasional stain.

Living Rooms

*Unwind in a room decorated in harmonious colors
and furnished with the easiest of easy chairs.*

▲ Sitting pretty

Plenty of seating makes a welcoming living
room, implying there's lots of space for visitors.
Several chairs can provide more seating than a
couple of sofas as, generally, only two people
will be able to sit comfortably and have a
conversation on a three-seater sofa.

◄ Easy cottage style

Rooms with exposed beams lend themselves
to relaxed country style with cotton-covered
upholstery and plenty of floral interest.

◄◄ Relaxed in cream

This room, which opens into the garden, has a
sunny, welcoming feel. The unusual bookshelves
with small compartments alternating with
larger ones, means that treasured items can be
displayed among the books without being
swamped by their surroundings.

The Art of Relaxation

A living room is nothing if it's not relaxing. It should be the place where you can unwind when work is over, kick off your shoes, slump on the sofa, enjoy a good book, watch your favorite TV program, pet the cat, share a glass of wine with friends, play a board game with the kids, or whatever else comes high on your indoor leisure list. While we might like to aspire to hotel lounge formality, worrying about keeping the house in sparkling order is the antithesis of family relaxation. That does not mean that when we're at home our living rooms have to descend into chaos. No, home relaxation is more about building easy-clean, instant-tidying into the original design and thinking about the overall harmony of the scheme.

Harmonious colors: Relaxing color schemes are generally those that are easy on the eye—neutrals, pastels, or deep moody shades, rather than those that are strongly contrasting in either color or tone. Large swathes of the more invigorating hot hues,

▶ **Lofty life**

Attic rooms are relaxing almost by definition. The quirky roof space usually precludes formality, and never more so than here, where roof struts are also part of the room architecture. Easy sofas with plenty of scatter cushions invite relaxation.

▼ **Sit back**

Relaxed doesn't have to mean disheveled, as demonstrated by this very pretty conservatory-inspired room. Plenty of cushions piled into the wicker chairs, green plants, and accessories ensure a sense of calm.

such as red, orange, or fuchsia, are unlikely to result in a relaxing scheme. That is not to say there are any colors you can't use—it's more a case of tempering them for a more harmonious look. If you love browns, for example, the addition of some burnt orange could be glorious because it brings life to the scheme, but is tonally close to earthy colors.

Easy care: Having a relaxed living room that is easy to clean does not have to mean compromising your style. When it comes to planning for instant tidying, steer clear of too many cluttering ornaments, which demand constant dusting and arranging. Instead, aim for plenty of cushions (with removable covers) that are quickly plumped up for a cozy look that invites relaxation. Living room mess often comes down to disorderly books, magazines, CDs, videos, and DVDs—so make sure you can quickly shut them behind closed doors in a tidy fashion on shelves suitably spaced to suit their proportions.

Creating the ambience: A relaxed living room is one that feels comfortable to you and reflects your style and personality. This is where detail counts. Decorative lighting is at its most useful in the living room. It not only creates mood, but the lamps themselves take on an almost sculptural element within the room, adding style. Fresh flowers are another way to create ambience, both for their decorative looks and because of their perfume. They are also an excellent way of bringing changes with the seasons, adding further personality to the room.

◀▲ Stylish storage

As well as comfortable seating, generous shelves are important in many living rooms, to keep books, CDs, and DVDs neat and close at hand.

◀ Lovely linen

Antique kitchen linen makes excellent furnishing fabric. Here, it has been used to cover a pretty tub chair and to lengthen navy blue drapes.

◀◀ Open solution

The open feel of this converted barn has been retained, so, instead of a series of rooms, the single space has been "zoned" with furniture.

Comfortable Seating

Wonderful plush sofas and chairs create a comfortable ambience in the sitting room. Allow for at least enough seats to accommodate the whole family and preferably more to welcome visitors. It is best to choose classic upholstery that will not date and add comfort with the seasonal style of cushions and throws. Use neatly piped cushions for a city-smart look, or large squashy ones with lively trimmings for a fun, relaxed style. Throws can be used to protect furniture against stains, as well as for extra color.

While a matching suite looks neat and cohesive, don't feel that you have to be tied by this. Two beautiful sofas that team rather than match, for example, can result in an interesting, individual living room.

▶ **Easy squeezy**

Soft white or cream leather is irresistibly plush, seriously chic, and yet remarkably maintenance-free, as it resists everyday grime and small spills can be mopped up quickly.

▼ **Pretty in pink**

Elegant upholstery in palest pink and white, in a style that is reminiscent of Louis XIV, adds a feeling of formality to this room. Fitted covers in pastel shades are best kept for livng rooms in a child-free zone.

TAKE ONE ROOM:
Pretty Living

Light and pretty, this sophisticated yellow, pink, and green scheme is inspired by the colors in the sofa upholstery fabric. This is always a clever way to build up interesting interiors. Start with the patterned fabric, and you should be able to find a wide choice of plain ones for the chairs, which can also be coordinated into the overall scheme. Paint colors come last, as they are available literally in the thousands, and if you can't find what you want in the swatches, have them computer-matched at the paint mixer. All you have to do is take along some of the fabric and ask the attendant to scan the color you want. The computer will break down the color into its components and then automatically mix the exact shade.

In this room, every detail is taken care of—even the flowers coordinate with the pink of the fabric.

Let professional designers inspire interesting color schemes by picking out a beautiful fabric, then matching the different shades for walls and upholstery.

REFERENCE POINT

■ Use pattern wisely and the result is one of cohesion; use it in an ill-informed way and your restful room turns into a place that is far from relaxing. See pages 38–41 for advice.

■ It is essential that you get your lighting right in the living room. Standard and table lamps are extremely useful, as they can be moved around until it is just right. See pages 146–153 for some helpful hints.

Yellow walls provide a strong but easy-to-live-with background color for a living room. In this one, the lampshades have been matched to the dominant color to strengthen the whole scheme.

Decorative lighting is a key player in living rooms. Both beautiful and useful, it can stamp your personality on the room while having a practical role to play. This pair of large lamps adds height to the whole interior.

Individual items of upholstered furniture can be far more stylish than a perfectly matching set. The trick is to keep all the pieces in proportion to each other.

This beautiful floral carpet has been specially woven to coordinate with the upholstery. An alternative would be to choose either a wooden floor or cream carpet with an added plain or bold modern rug that picks out one or more of the colors from the scheme.

ART AT AUCTION 1983–84

VAN GOGH

Kitchens

Welcome to the heart of the home, a room that is so much more than a food factory—enter, relax, and be entertained.

▲ Minimum requirements

A stove, sink, refrigerator, and a couple of cupboards are all you need to make a kitchen. Here, the bare necessities fit into a length of less than eight feet.

◀ Citrus style

Citrus shades are happy colors to live with—a good choice for the kitchen, where we spend so much time. The striking lemon-yellow bar stools add both a relaxed living element and an exciting sculptural edge.

◀◀ Light and dark

Dark cupboards, floors, and tiled walls provide a strong contrast with the white wall cupboards. This combination works because the tones are designed as blocks of color and the glass-fronted cupboards, being higher, emulate windows.

Kitchen Planning

Kitchens are fast becoming the main living room of the home, and many now include an eating area (even if it's only a breakfast bar), and even a seating space. When planning your kitchen, these are considerations that need to be taken into account.

First things first: Decide on your kitchen lifestyle. If yours is a purely adult household and no-fuss meals are your style, then a compact corner kitchen could be right for you. However, families may prefer to aim for one-room living that includes dining, lounge seating, even a TV corner. If you don't have a huge area, don't write off this option, as it's surprising how much can fit into a small space. Decide which part of the room will house the kitchen area and how it will work with the rest. Do you want an island unit or a breakfast bar, for example, so you can prepare food without having your back to everyone else in the room?

▶ Good planning
Most of the working area of this kitchen is along one wall, which accommodates the sink and cooking area. An eye-level stove and refrigerator are on the adjacent wall, making the ideal work triangle.

▼ Great galleys
Narrow galley kitchens are great work spaces, as everything is within reach and there's little need for movement between sink, stove, and refrigerator. The stools at the end of this room allow for casual conversations to continue while the chef creates a masterpiece.

Work triangle: Efficient kitchens are ergonomically designed to allow for easy food preparation. Put simply, it means you need to aim for a triangle between the three principal work areas: food storage, cooking, and washing up, with adequate preparation areas in between. This "triangle" could be in a straight line, if that is the design of your kitchen, but all the elements need to be within easy reach of each other and unbroken by a doorway, which could mean constant interruption to the smooth operation of food preparation.

In a large kitchen-dining area, you may decide to put the kitchen just along one wall. Alternatively, you may decide to combine the triangle and eating area in an island unit, which doubles up on eating and preparation space and incorporates, for example, an under-worktop dishwasher opposite the main group of units.

▲ Square's fair

A square kitchen is easy to work in, especially if the triangle is arranged along two adjacent walls. If you love the idea of a central kitchen table, beware of arranging the triangle on three walls near the table, as you'll spend your time walking around it.

◄ On the move

This black and yellow kitchen is hardly huge, yet it provides ample space for both food preparation and dining. The central table is on wheels and so, when necessary, can be moved to one side for ease of access.

Kitchen Living

As modern kitchens shed their functional image and become more and more of a general living space, so their design is changing. On the one hand, they're taking on a softer, more comfortable look; on the other, they are becoming the showcase of the house. The trend is moving from a fully fitted kitchen to one that is more domestic and informal. Ovens are less likely to be built-in and wall mounted and more likely to be range style. Kitchen cupboards (if there are any) will possibly be confined to one wall, while a beautiful piece of furniture (perhaps antique) may be used elsewhere in the room for storage with a more decorative feel. There's a growing demand for dining space within the kitchen, and builders are starting to factor this in to new houses, sometimes even dispensing with the dining room altogether in favor of open-plan kitchen living.

▲ In the round

Round tables provide more comfortable seating in small areas. They are also excellent pieces of furniture in kitchens, as they break up the otherwise naturally rectangular look of cupboards, stoves, refrigerators, and freezers.

▲ Appealing drapes

A cool white drape fitted to a rod on the ceiling allows for versatile kitchen living. Most of the time, it is pulled back for an open-plan space with plenty of room for dining. However, when entertaining, the hostess can pull the drape across to hide the fallout from food preparation.

◀ Long story

There's plenty of dining space in this long kitchen, with the table running parallel to a neatly fitted cooking area, which even incorporates a built-in television. The lighting helps to define the eating area.

Kitchen Storage

In the kitchen, good storage is everything. As the Shakers used to believe, there should be "a place for everything, and everything in its place," to make work more efficient, eliminate the need to search for things, and make cleaning up easier. Plan the storage so everything is as close as possible to where you need it. It might sound obvious, but if the pans, herbs, spices, and cooking condiments are near to the stove, you will be saved a surprising amount of preparation time and, depending on the size of your kitchen, energy. Likewise, store coffee, tea, sugar, and even cups near the kettle for a quick brew, and china and glass near the dishwasher for instant unloading. Chopping boards and knives need to be stored both close to each other and near the preparation area.

▶ On display

Old-fashioned kitchen cupboards were used both to store crockery and for display. The shelves of this piece are being used purely for the latter.

◀▼ Airspace

Not everything has to be locked away inside cupboards. A ceiling-hung frame buys extra space to store bulky items, such as pans, which are then within easy reach of the cooking area.

▼ Transparent solution

If you love to display your favorite things, but prefer to spare them the inevitable layer of kitchen grease, then glass-fronted wall cupboards are the perfect solution.

◄◄ Dressing up

Beautiful pieces of white china and porcelain deserve to be shown off, and there's little that can do this better than the time-honored cupboard. If the china is used regularly (and, therefore, frequently washed), and the cupboard is not positioned too near the stove, kitchen grime should not be an issue.

◄ Miscellanea

The display on your kitchen cupboard does not have to be a coordinated collection of china or glass; it can be a more personal mix of treasured items.

▼ Hang up

If you don't have the cupboard space, hang up whatever you can. Most kitchen utensils and pots have a hole at the end of the handle, and can be hung up by a butcher's hook.

As well as designing storage zones, plan the kind of cupboards and storage space that will be useful for the size and shape of their contents. Most cupboards come with adjustable shelving so, for example, you may want to put three shelves into a cupboard for mugs and only two for stacks of large serving dishes. Spice jars are no good jumbling around in a large cupboard, but with labeled tops and stacked in a shallow drawer, they are much easier to pick out.

There are many kitchen drawer and cupboard interiors that are specially designed for different uses. They can be expensive, so think very carefully about what would really suit you before buying. From an esthetic point of view, decide whether you want everything behind doors or whether you'd prefer open shelving that can store quick-to-reach casseroles or bowls, which are also good to look at and pleasant to display.

TAKE ONE ROOM:
Open-Plan Kitchen

A light, bright kitchen that opens into other rooms is a pleasant and sociable working area. Cooking and preparation continues, even after guests have arrived, and the hosts can enjoy the company, too. When well planned, this arrangement does not have to look functional, and with so many exquisite kitchen fittings nowadays, this is the room that invariably attracts the most investment in a modern home. Units can be confined to one wall or arranged in a U-shape, as here, yet still allow plenty of space for dining. This kitchen demonstrates how, with the clever addition of sliding walls, the space can become even more flexible: in turns opening into a formal dining space, or being confined to the cooking and informal eating area.

Either use the same floor throughout to link all the areas of an open-plan kitchen-diner, or use different types of flooring to delineate different areas. For example, you may use practical, water-resistant stone or slate at the cooking end, and a softer-looking wood in the areas where you relax.

Sliding walls offer versatile kitchen living. They are pulled back most of the time for an open-plan look but, when guests arrive, they can be closed to conceal kitchen clutter.

REFERENCE POINT

■ It is the finer details that say so much about a room. In the kitchen, the faucets that you choose for your sink will add to the room's style. See pages 114–115 for everything you need to know about the subject.

■ A hardwearing flooring is a must. For more help with your decision, see the choices on pages 78–85.

Spotlights provide ideal kitchen background lighting. Whether you choose recessed, track, or wire mounted lights, it is important to install enough to ensure that adequate light reaches all areas of the working kitchen. The number of fittings you use will depend on whether they are low voltage or high voltage and the light output of each fitting. Your supplier or electrician will be able to advise you.

Flush-fronted wooden cupboards are stylish, durable, and, in the case of the peninsular unit that houses the stove, almost take on the role of a wall.

Sliding walls can be used to divide the kitchen from the formal eating area. However, unless the family is entertaining, these are usually kept open to create a large, light, open-plan living area.

An informal eating area allows plenty of space for family meals. The round table makes a pleasant contrast with the more angular units.

A stone-tiled floor throughout is very practical and unifies the kitchen-dining room.

Dining Rooms

Create a convivial dining room by exploring your more adventurous tendencies, then add flexibility with changes of table dressings.

▲ Mixed and matched

Disparate junk-shop chairs look remarkably elegant when they are all covered in a matching heavy white cotton and set around a long oval table.

◀▲ Cream dream

Always elegant, cream has timeless appeal, as demonstrated by this contemporary dining room, which has encompassed tradition with an over-the-mantel oil painting.

◀ Style simplicity

Simple, modern, wooden dining furniture provides excellent dining flexibility, as the shapes do not make too strong a statement in themselves. Minimal as this room is, it can take on very different looks with the addition of tablecloths and an attractive table setting.

◀◀ Color story

Bright colors have a strong tradition in dining rooms, creating an intimate mood. An extrovert yellow, like this, works well both during the day and in the evening when the lights are low.

Formal vs Informal Dining

You can afford to be adventurous in dining rooms because they are generally designed to be hospitable and are not necessarily required to be relaxing in the same way as living rooms.

Clever color: In dining rooms, you can be confident about using good strong color because while in most rooms the furniture is arranged around the walls, here the walls are often clutter-free. Traditionally, vivid wall colors, such as deep green or magenta, were most frequently used. Nowadays, however, lighter, brighter color schemes are to the fore, and striking pieces of artwork used to good effect.

When setting the table for informal occasions, pick out these colors with inexpensive table linens, which can be changed to suit

▶ **Setting the scene**

Tablecloths can be magical transformers. A small, square table has been enlarged with the addition of a removable round tabletop, then covered with a rich brown cloth to set off the golden-yellow walls. The choice of lemon-yellow china and flowers unites the setting in one cheerful whole.

▼ **Natural expression**

This dining area adjoins the kitchen and yet is divided from the worst excesses of food preparation by a sleek, doorless partition. The unusual rush chairs, although a contemporary design, have a timeless feel. Their shape makes a bold statement, but their color teams well with almost any shade in the décor.

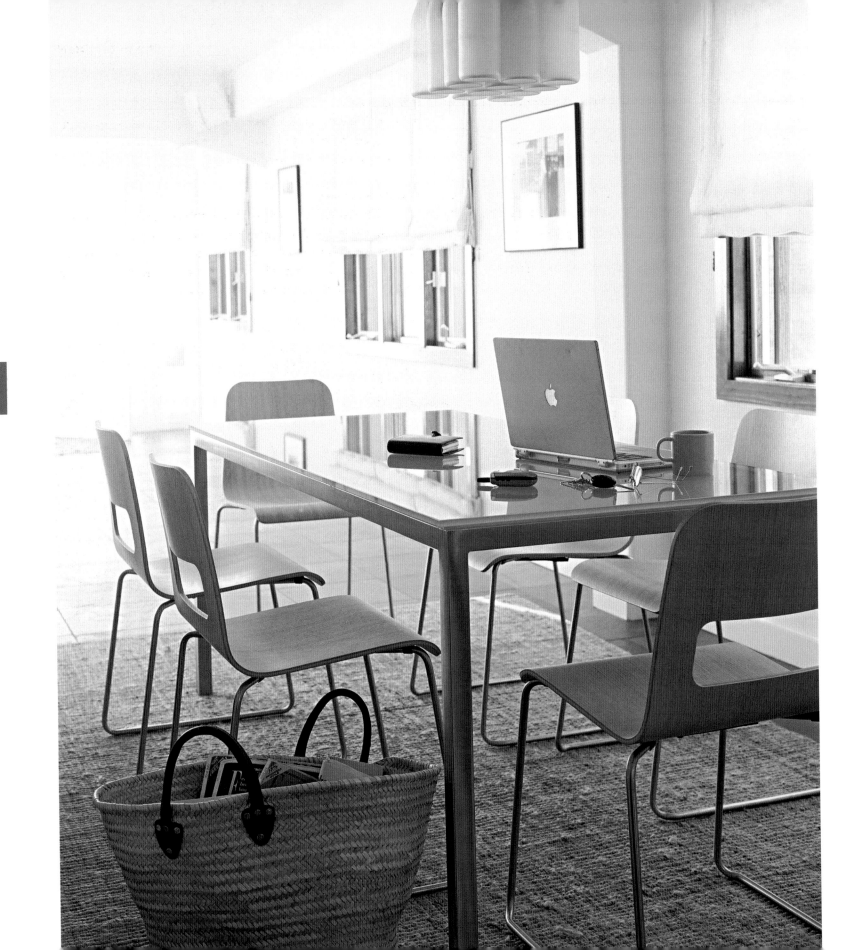

the season. For formal occasions, white is always elegant and will complement any scheme.

Light fantastic: Ambience is everything in the dining room, so plan for versatile lighting. Spotlights with dimmer switches are useful, but supplement them with something more dramatic, such as a directional spotlight highlighting a focal point. While wall sconces add mood, central pendants or chandeliers are the best way to introduce light over the table—use dimmer switches so they don't dazzle the diners, and make sure they hang above the sight line. All this, of course, can be supplemented by the most romantic light of all—candlelight.

◀ White light

White walls, plenty of natural light, and a glass-topped table—these are all the ingredients of a light and airy contemporary look, which is conducive to both work and relaxation.

▼ Old meets new

Clean white walls set off a long refectory table and chairs, which exude an almost medieval feel, making a curious but successful combination of old and new. The wrought-iron chandelier above the table furthers the theme of times past, as it is lit by candles rather than electricity. At night, the light in this dining room will be subtle and romantic.

TAKE ONE ROOM:
Cool Dining Room

More often than not, the dining table is in the center, which not only takes the focus away from the walls, but means you can make use of areas that do not have much wall space, such as a wide hallway or corridor. This dining room has at least two doorways, which would make it unsuitable for most other uses, yet the finished look is very pleasing indeed. The very fact that the focus is always on the table, which almost "floats" in the middle of the room, means that this room feels light and airy. The glass tabletop accentuates this, especially when the dining room is not in use, as visually the table almost disappears. As well as its own intrinsic beauty, it also shows off the exquisite chairs, which can be seen in their entirety, even when neatly pushed under the table.

A table and chairs is all you need for a dining area. If you can't set aside a whole room, make use of lobbies or circulation areas within other rooms.

REFERENCE POINT

■ Flooring in a dining room can be any material, as long as it complements the rest of the setting. Under a table, it should be easy to clean. See pages 76–91 for your choices.

■ The dining room can be the perfect place to explore more unusual color schemes. See pages 32–41 for practical advice and pages 46–57 for some inspirational ideas from other people's homes.

A confident, modern painting takes center stage in an all-white painted room. This picture, in charcoal gray, is in keeping with the room's monochromatic theme. An alternative, brightly colored one would be just as effective.

An etched-glass screen, set at an angle against the window, adds an extra dimension to the room. It softens the daylight and also gives an otherwise utilitarian window a little more glamor.

Beautiful modern wooden chairs have been elegantly worked to become sculptures in themselves, adding to the style of the room.

The glass-topped table has a translucency that is airy during the day but becomes more moody at night as the glass reflects the shadows.

Bedrooms

Of all the rooms in the house, you can be most self-indulgent in your bedroom—your own private sanctuary.

▲ Details that count

Potted plants not only look lovely in bedrooms, but, if they're highly scented like this hyacinth, they have a glorious fresh perfume that's a delight to wake up to.

◄ Country style

Pretty in pink and white, this ultrafeminine, country-style bedroom has fresh appeal, mainly because the pattern has not been overdone. With plenty of white, including the drapes, the overall look is light and airy.

◄◄ Timeless design

This traditional French-style bedroom still holds much appeal. The wooden headboard is upholstered in a pretty blue and cream fabric, which is complemented by the canopy. The beautiful lace-edged linen adds a feminine touch.

Restful Style

Decorating your bedroom is all about creating an ambience where you can truly relax and unwind at the end of the day. This is the place where you can please yourself and indulge your own personal style, free from the practical needs (and tastes) of the rest of the family.

Restful shades: It is generally accepted that the bedroom is a predominantly feminine room—even if a man is one of the sleeping partners. This means that it is possible to use pretty pastels and patterns in ways that might not be in keeping with the rest of the house. Soft, harmonious combinations in sugar-almond shades, such as pinks, blues, aquas, or yellows, create a relaxing atmosphere that has remained in favor since the days of the eighteenth-century Parisian boudoirs. Alternatively, you may

▲ All white

You can't go wrong with an all-white room. It's peaceful and relaxing, and you can mix new and antique linen. Collect wonderful old sheets and pillowcases trimmed with lace or monogrammed to add a special touch.

◄◄▲ Tall order

A four-poster bed, be it traditional or modern, will always provide a focal point in the room and require very little else around it. The canopy provides an intimate feel, not only because it forms a private "den," but because the shadows it casts affect the light.

◄ Color story

Many midtones are excellent for bedrooms. This vibrant aqua brings daytime brightness to a simple room and, at night, a rich background glow.

◄◄ Twin style

White and cream add up to a timelessly elegant bedroom, furnished with beautiful French-style twin beds, which set the mood for the room.

prefer to go for intimate dark and sultry schemes inspired by *The Arabian Nights,* with deep reds, plums, or purples, highlighted with gold—all of which look best after dark.

Flexible pattern: There's plenty of scope for pattern in the bedroom as bed linens join forces with fabrics and wallpapers to widen your choices. You could go for a fully coordinated look or, if you prefer to be more restrained, you could put together an elegant, plain color scheme and simply add pattern with bed linen, which can be changed with the seasons.

Whatever scheme you choose, it is important to pin up large swatches of your chosen paint colors and fabrics to see how they look together, both by daylight and by lamplight.

Lighting for mood: Creating ambience all comes down to lighting, and in the bedroom you need a combination of both mood lighting and directional light (from a bedside lamp or spotlight, for example), which provides enough light for reading. Pretty table lamps and wall sconces have an important role to play in the interior design of bedrooms, both for the light they emit and for their sculptural appeal. Even if the rest of the decoration is a little disparate, the introduction of a pair of beautiful lamps, one on each side of the bed, immediately introduces cohesion and style to the room.

◀▲ Old charm

A glorious heirloom quilt is given a crisp new look with clean white scalloped linen. The red background fabric of the quilt has been picked up by the room's occupant, who has painted the metal bedstead red to match—an excellent example of attention to detail.

◀ Passing pattern

Delightful blue and white checkered bed linen teams well with the striped floorcloth, introducing an element of pattern to the bedroom. Keep the look fresh by interchanging them with pretty blue and white floral bed linen, for example.

◀◀ Sheer touch

A length of diaphanous sheer fabric, pinned to wires strung from the ceiling, adds an ethereal touch to the simplest of summer-home bedrooms. The transparent fabric diffuses daylight as it floods into the room, and at night the oil lamp suspended from one of the rafters introduces yet more romantic lighting.

Beds & Headboards

The bed is the *raison d'être* of the bedroom and is always an important feature. So select it with care to ensure both a comfortable night's sleep and to set the style of the room. Whether you choose to make your bed with a single pillow or pile it high with cushions galore, it is still the type of bed that will determine the character of the room.

Start by deciding whether you want a divan, which would necessitate a valance for cover, or whether you prefer an airier look, with legs on display. Generally, if you choose a divan, you can change the headboard later if you wish. Beds on legs without valances are less solid, but the headboards and bedsteads are part of the frame and are impossible to change.

Headboards generally fall into into three categories: metal, which looks light and airy; wood, for a structured feel; or sumptuous upholstery. For a more substantial finish, look to antique French- or Swedish-style headboards, which often combine a wooden frame with an upholstered interior.

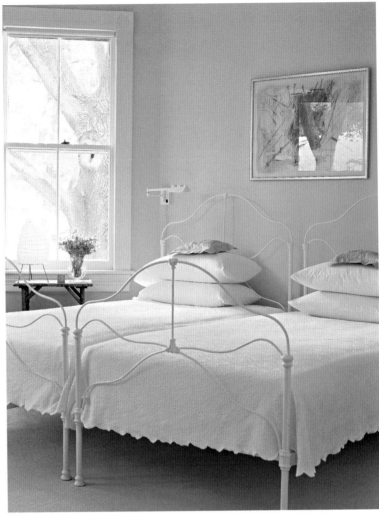

▲ Antique metal

White-painted antique metal bedheads are one of the prettiest styles, bringing a light and feminine touch to a bedroom. There is also a wide choice of metal-framed beds, which come in several finishes, ranging from gun metal to chrome, and a selection of powder-coated colors.

◀ Carved wood

Carved wooden frames can be very spectacular—some reach over six feet high. An antique wooden headboard fixed to a modern divan bring style and stature to any bedroom, be it period or indisputably modern, as is the case here.

210

▲ Padded comfort

Padded headboards have their origins in French and Swedish upholstered, wood-framed headboards. They became very popular in the twentieth century, offering plenty of comfort and a sumptuous feel.

◄▲ Painted wood

Popularized by classic Swedish style, painted headboards have a simple charm that suits both modern and period homes. The bonus is that they can quickly be given a new look with a fresh coat of paint.

◄ Rococo style

Pretty, shaped, rococo-style headboards look delightful painted white with gold detail and softened with many, variously sized, pillows. This is all you need for a focal point in a pure white bedroom.

Bedroom Storage

The main challenge in modern bedrooms is how to fit it all in. These are the rooms that have often been shrunk in today's houses in favor of extra bathrooms and capacious living space. To exacerbate the situation, there is more to fit in: a larger bed, a television and/or music center; plus plenty of room is needed to accommodate clothes, shoes, accessories, spare comforters, books, jewelry, and face creams. The key is adequate storage.

You can never have too many bedroom closets, and in response to this, modern cabinet manufacturers have come up with ingenious bedroom storage systems that are specially divided to accommodate the varying scale of our storage needs, thus helping our bedrooms to be freed of clutter and furnished with just one or two beautiful pieces. Painted junk-shop furniture, such as a pretty chair or little chest, can neatly add ambience.

212

◀ Double deal

This beautiful antique chest provides both bedside table and bedroom storage. It's perfect for hiding away all those lotions, potions, and creams that have a habit of littering bedroom surfaces.

◀◀ Period solution

Freestanding antique armoires have an appeal all their own with their period style. They have become increasingly popular and can look very good in a modern setting, especially if they're painted white or cream.

◀◀◀ Perfect order

Modern, fitted wall-to-wall cupboards can be craftily designed so they are disguised as the wall itself. Behind the doors, they can be organized with shelves, shoe cubbyholes, and hanging space, providing ample room to accommodate your whole wardrobe.

The Linen Cupboard

There's something immensely satisfying about sheets, all neatly laundered, scented, and piled up in the linen cupboard. Traditional, stand-alone linen cupboards were known as linen presses. They still make attractive bedroom cupboards, suitable for folded clothes, as well as linen. Nowadays, the linen cupboard is just as likely to be modern and built in, but the principle is the same. For quick selection, allow different shelves for single and double sheets. Alternatively, color code the linens, for example, using pretty pastels for the children's singles, crisp white for your doubles. Keep pillowcases, singles, doubles, and quilt covers in separate piles, to prevent them toppling over.

▶ Showing off

By stacking pillowcases frill-side out, you don't have to keep pulling them out and unfolding them to discover the ones you want. Piled in color coordinated stacks, they are pleasing to the eye and allow easy selection when it comes to changing the sheets.

▼ Stealing space

Here, the narrow space behind the door, unusable for much else, has been turned into shelving to accommodate the household linen. Neatly stacked in bedlinen sizes, the sheets, quilt covers, and pillowcases are easy to find.

214

▲ Florals and geometrics

When it comes to mixing patterns, florals and stripes always make a good team as the designs work together, rather than fighting against each other. The color coordination works best if you keep to a color theme and bear in mind the scale. Small florals look best with fine stripes, more flamboyant designs with bolder geometrics.

TAKE ONE ROOM:

No-Fuss Bedroom

Period or modern, a four-poster bed is so imposing, it would not matter if it were the sole piece of furniture in the bedroom. However, this one in pale gray metal is striking without being heavy or hard, and its pale color makes for easy color coordination. Here, it tonally provides a link between the lemon yellow and rather stronger-colored bed linen. This four-poster has no drapes, providing a no-fuss modern look.

If you prefer a more feminine feel, furnish a bed such as this with pretty gathered drapes, in traditional style, or keep it modern with a sheer panel draped down the back and across the top with a short overhang at the front. It would look wonderful in a white sheer; or you could add interest with color. Remember that as it is translucent, the sheer would look much paler when held against the light. Sheer panels also affect the ambience of a room as they gently blow in the lightest breeze.

Bed linen brings versatile color and pattern to the bedroom as it can be changed easily to suit the seasons and even to completely update the room.

REFERENCE POINT

■ In this room the window is dressed with fresh white Roman shades. For more shades, see pages 132–135. If you like other modern window dressings, see pages 128–131, and, for something traditional, see pages 124–127.

■ To make the bed even more luxurious, add a throw and some decorative cushions. See the advice given on pages 144–145.

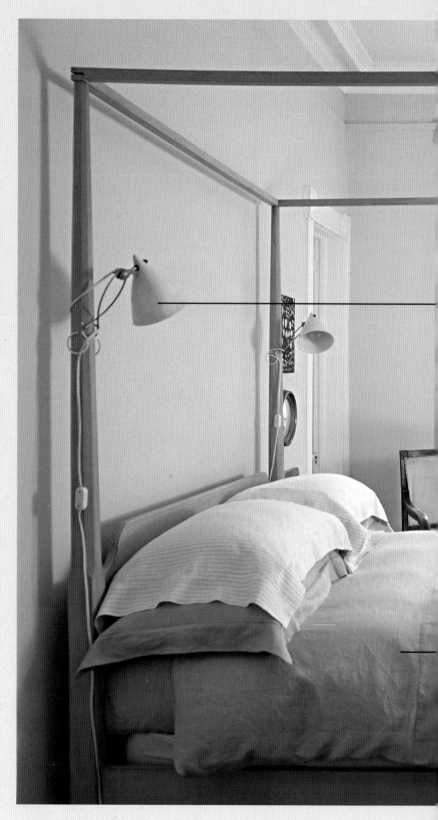

Simple white Roman shades make a clean, modern window treatment that works equally well at the window and the French doors.

Bed-mounted spotlights are excellent reading lights and keep the look modern and unfussy.

Lemon-yellow walls are fresh and relaxing, perfectly complementing the outdoor feel of this garden room.

Four-posters don't have to be period style. Modern, metal-framed four-posters like this one make just as much of an impact on a room, yet are less imposing.

Bold ikat-style stripes in aqua and green add fresh modern pattern to a plain interior. When you change the sheets, keep up the interest by changing the design for something completely different. Choose a light and sunny look for the summer, for example, and wonderful russet shades for the fall.

Bathrooms

Whatever your preference in bathroom design, there's a wide choice available in creating your ideal home spa.

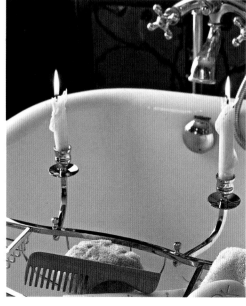

◀◀◀ Tile alternatives

In decorative terms, ceramic tiles offer endless scope—not just in their color, shape, and size, but also in the ways they can be put up. These brick-shaped white and green tiles, for example, have been laid diagonally for a stunning zigzag effect.

◀◀ Modern spa

Clean white tiles and a wall of glass bricks combine to make the most luxurious of modern home spas. The sunken bath also becomes a step-in shower, giving plenty of room for maneuvering.

◀ Freestanding style

The demand for original Victorian clawfoot bathtubs in the last decade has prompted designers to come up with modern equivalents. This design marries curviness with a strongly geometric bathroom design. Good-looking from all angles, it would have worked just as well in the center of the room.

◀◀◀ Home sanctuary

Decorate the bathroom to create a relaxing ambience, so even if time and resources won't allow for treats, there is always the bath to luxuriate in. Light some candles, add luxury bath oils, lie back, and relax.

Bathroom Basics

Even if it is the smallest room in the house, the bathroom can be the most expensive to equip per square foot, so it is important not to scrimp on planning time.

Find your style: Do you love the look of pretty, Victorian-style bathrooms with clawfoot bathtubs, etched glass, and flamboyant brassware? Do you prefer a more contemporary built-in look, or are you captivated by modern minimalism? Spend time researching what is available before you even begin planning.

Planning priorities: The size of your bathroom and positioning of pipes may restrict its layout. If you're starting from scratch, plan for ducting and possibly a raised floor to conceal the pipe work, toilet tank, and under-floor heating. With all this in place, if you have a choice, put the more beautiful pieces at focal points—the toilet never looks gorgeous, so don't make it the first item you see when you open the bathroom door.

Floor options: Bathroom floors should be waterproof. You can use hard flooring such as ceramic tiles or stone, but bamboo is the only suitable wood. All of these are designed as part of the architecture, should be expected to last many years, and need to be laid before the bathroom fixtures are put in. Most sheet flooring is suitable, notably rubber, vinyl, and rubber-backed carpet

▲ **Bygone beauty**

The appeal of a Victorian clawfoot bathtub has never completely waned and, indeed, in recent years it has seen a revival. Choose Victorian-style pillar taps or Victorian-style single-faucet units with shower handsets to team with the bath.

◀ **Modern style**

Bathrooms have turned a corner in recent years, some taking their influence from Japanese style with square or rectangular basins that sit on the worktops. Set on a mosaic-tiled unit, the effect here is that of East meets West. Exposed wicker baskets make attractive storage.

◀◀ **Twice as nice**

Double basins add a sense of luxury, and are a civilized way to reduce bathroom traffic in the morning. This workbench style with exposed storage under the basins is very twenty-first century, as is the generous walk-in shower.

specially designed for bathrooms. The flooring should be laid after the fixtures are in position.

Wall wisdom: Ceramic, glass, or stone tiles are the most obvious waterproof choice, offering plenty of scope in terms of color and design, ranging from tiny ceramics to huge two-foot-square slabs. If you prefer paint, choose an eggshell finish, which is splashproof and can be wiped clean. It won't last as long as ceramic tiles, but it is easy to recoat and could be covered with a glass panel if desired.

▲ In a pretty cabinet

If you have room for freestanding furniture, it makes a delightful personal touch in the bathroom. This antique French cupboard perfectly sets off the more lovely bathroom paraphernalia.

◄ Freestanding luxury

When baths are placed in the middle of the floor, you will need floor-mounted taps, and the neatest way to fit these is to run the pipes under a raised floor.

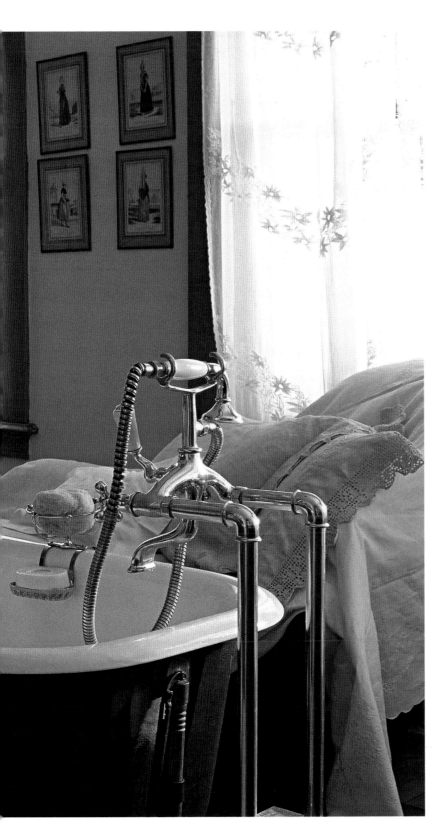

Bathroom Storage

The key to a beautiful bathroom is plenty of storage, some of which is designed to display, and some to conceal. All the gorgeous things—bath oils, soaps, shampoos, and fluffy towels—give personality to a bathroom and look good on display. But there's also plenty that is far from lovely, and to keep the bathroom looking good, you need to be able to quickly hide these away. Think about the scale of the storage. Small things need to be on narrow shelves so everything is within easy reach and doesn't get lost in the melee of bathroom minutiae. Toilet paper, cleaning equipment, bathmats, and towels, on the other hand, will need capacious closets.

▲ **Neat move**
An alcove running the length of the bath has been lined with the same white tiles that run around the room, creating an accessible and yet understated storage shelf.

▲ Full to the brim

A charming little chest, chock-full of tiny drawers, is a delightful way to store small bathroom items like tooth-cleaning kits, medicines, and bandages. When each item has its own drawer, it will be easy to find—and easy to put away, too.

◄ Creative corridor

Capacious closets located just outside the bathroom must be the greatest luxury. This has been achieved here by stealing a little width off the corridors to give plenty of space for storing towels and other bulky requisites.

TAKE ONE ROOM:

Furnishing the Bathroom

Since only the wealthiest of Victorian homes had bathrooms with running water, many present owners of period houses set aside a small bedroom for the purpose. This is often far more roomy than bathrooms in modern homes, giving plenty of space for a more informal look. This bathroom, for example, has been furnished in a similar way to other rooms in the house, with a cabinet for storage and display, and wall-mounted lights and mirror, and other pretty touches, such as the little upholstered stool and displayed bathroom objects on the cabinet top. By avoiding shiny tiles, the whole room retains a soft, furnished look, and the eggshell white paint is both splashproof and quick and easy to retouch to keep it looking neat.

Modern houses are more likely to have fully installed bathrooms, though the trend is returning to a more casual look, made possible by new, freestanding bath designs and clever concealment of pipes and tanks.

Victorian-style bathrooms with clawfoot bathtubs are often more informal, a style that has now become popular in modern homes too.

REFERENCE POINT

■ Read up on bathroom fixtures on pages 116–121 before choosing what suits you and your bathroom best. Faucets are covered on pages 116–117, sinks on 118–119, and showers on pages 120–121.

■ Radiators and heated towel rails are also essential in the bathroom for the ultimate in coziness—see pages 112–113.

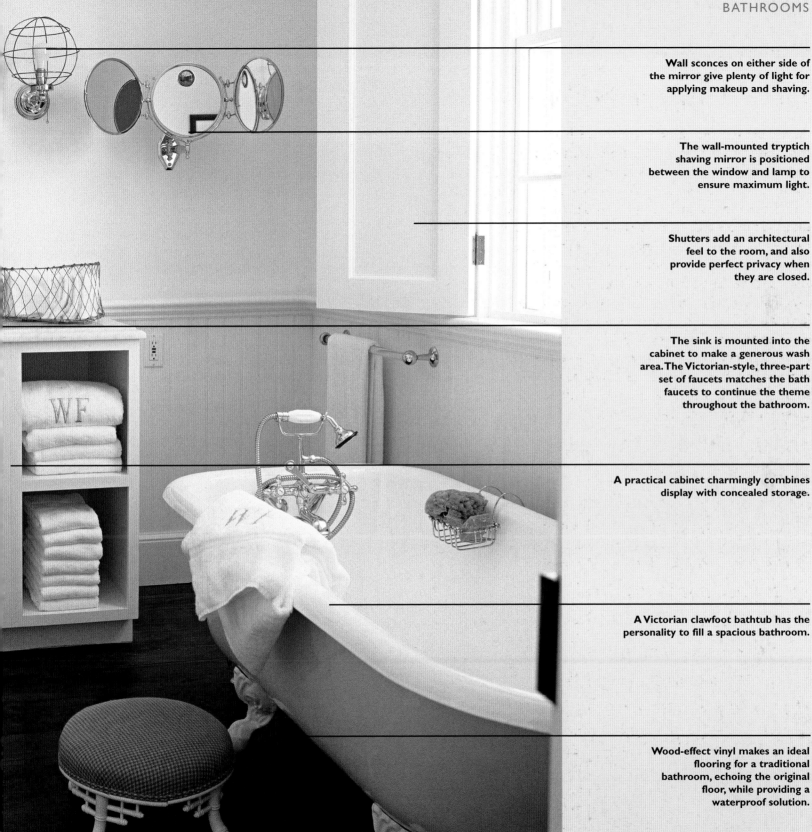

Wall sconces on either side of the mirror give plenty of light for applying makeup and shaving.

The wall-mounted tryptich shaving mirror is positioned between the window and lamp to ensure maximum light.

Shutters add an architectural feel to the room, and also provide perfect privacy when they are closed.

The sink is mounted into the cabinet to make a generous wash area. The Victorian-style, three-part set of faucets matches the bath faucets to continue the theme throughout the bathroom.

A practical cabinet charmingly combines display with concealed storage.

A Victorian clawfoot bathtub has the personality to fill a spacious bathroom.

Wood-effect vinyl makes an ideal flooring for a traditional bathroom, echoing the original floor, while providing a waterproof solution.

Children's Rooms

Create a fun fantasy land or brightly colored den, which your children can make their own.

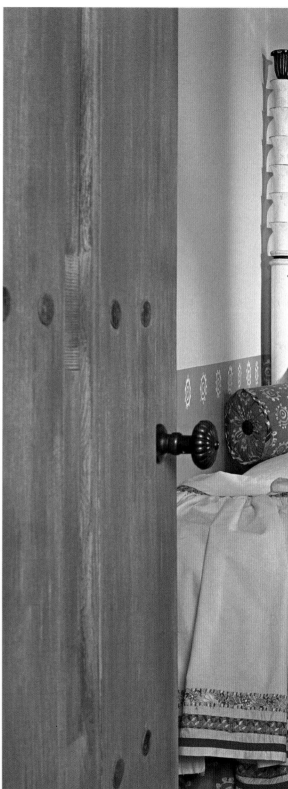

▲ Show off

Children are inveterate collectors, so it's a good idea to provide some attractive ways to display their trophies. This wall-mounted house-shaped trinket box shows off its contents for all to enjoy.

◀ Princess palace

Little girls just love to be princesses, so make them a royal bedroom, even if it's simply with the addition of a fancy headboard made from painted medium-density fiberboard. Lots of bulletin board and desk space also comes high on any child's priority list.

◀◀ Color it bright

Children love their rooms to be brightly colored, so furnish the room with child-sized furniture that is upholstered or painted in contrasting colors.

Clutter Control

Delight the children with a den of their own, full of exciting things to thrill and amuse them. They love to have themed rooms—of fairy castles, for example, underwater worlds, or featuring their favorite cartoon characters. Whatever they choose, however, the fantasy will be drowned by a deluge of toys unless the storage is sorted.

Storage priorities: Organize the toys into big boxes of large things, and smaller boxes of little things. Alternatively, you could use large boxes that hold several smaller boxes of similar-category toys. This is useful for art needs, for example with wax crayons in one small box, colored pencils in another, and stamps or stencils in another. All these can then be stacked into cupboards, onto shelves, or even under the bed. At bedtime, encourage children to help tidy up by, for example, suggesting they put all the cars in the car box or all the baby doll clothes in the dolls' closet, while you handle the more complicated sorting.

On the bed: By far the most important piece of furniture in a little girl's life is her bed. Girls love sleigh beds in pretty pastel shades, or four-poster "princess beds," though you can create a similar draped effect with mosquito netting hung over an ordinary bed.

For boys, make a brightly painted jungle, car, or train engine fantasy headboard, cut from wood. If the ceiling height allows it, choose a loft bed to save space. Children will love clambering up and down the ladder, and they'll have all that space underneath for a desk, a closet, or simply for play.

▲▶ Pastel perfection
Children respond to harmonious color schemes, making for peaceful bedtimes. This painted antique headboard makes a pretty starting point, with accessories in pink designed to complement the roses.

▶ Stylish storage
Plenty of storage keeps the clutter at bay. A large chest of drawers on each side of the bed encourages quick clean-up times.

▶▶ Going up
Bunk beds are the classic solution for children sharing a room as they allow maximum play space. This blue bunk introduces color to the room, matching the child-sized sofa.

TAKE ONE ROOM:

Compact Solution

Where space is limited, children's rooms can be made to work by stacking their personal items. They love to climb up a ladder to bed, so make the "air space" work. Here, an attic box room has been transformed into a magical bedroom suitable for any child old enough to sleep in a bunk, right up to the teenage years. The bed has been custom-made with drawers underneath to provide a surprising amount of storage while taking up minimal floor space—and there's still room for an upholstered chair next to the bed and space to play in.

When the child is young, the "capsule" can be painted to create a fantasy land, such as a princess's chamber, a fire engine, or an underwater wonderland. As they grow up, it can simply be repainted and given new bed linen to create a much more grown-up, teenage look, like this one. Let them add their own touches with posters; hooks to hang necklaces, bracelets, and bags; and strings of decorative lights.

Create a room out of almost nothing by custom building a capsule bedroom in the attic. By designing it to fit, you can make very efficient use of the space.

REFERENCE POINT

■ For other ideas on personalizing cushion covers, see pages 144–145.

■ Color is essential when decorating a child's bedroom or play area. See the advice on pages 32–35 before you start wielding your paintbrush.

■ Pattern, too, works wonders. For the best effects see pages 38–41.

232

Recessed spotlights provide ample light and sidestep the potential danger of lamps overturning in the night.

The whole "capsule" has been painted white to keep it looking clean and fresh and maximize the sense of space.

A shelf at the end of the bed provides extra storage for books or other small items.

Color-coordinated bedding and cushions create an inviting ambience. This bed is decorated for a young teenager, but it would be just as appealing for a younger child, especially when joined by her stuffed animal friends.

The bed has a fascia board built up into the eaves. This results in a cozy den, and makes the very best use of space.

Long, narrow drawers provide useful storage space as they can accommodate several piles of clothes or other items within their length. If tidiness isn't your child's strong point, insert drawer dividers or smaller boxes into each drawer.

An upholstered chair is useful for the younger years when children still enjoy listening to their parents reading stories (capsule space can be somewhat cramped if an adult joins in). As the child grows up, you may prefer to exchange this for a made-to-measure desk for arts and crafts and homework.

Home Offices

Keep papers under control in a well-organized home office—whether it be but a corner, or a whole room.

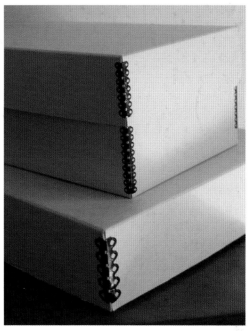

▲ File style

Stylish boxes that hold stationary and other paper goods can easily be put on display. By coordinating your choices with your room decor, you can create a sense of order and calm in the "paper mountain".

◄ Corner solution

Just a corner of this room has been set aside for office space. Tall filing cabinets, made of the same pale wood as the coffee table, give it a furnished look that is in keeping with the rest of the room.

◄◄ Organization space

You can never have enough office shelf space—the key to an efficient office is to allow enough shelving for all your filing and books. Here, bookshelves not only cover the walls, but run across the top of the door, too.

Office Order

With the arrival of the electronic age, home offices are taking on an increasing importance because of the growing number of people who are choosing to work from home. That aside, the business side of running a home requires plenty of filing space, as the promise of the "paperless office" is yet to arrive—if, indeed, it ever does.

A place for everything: Internet banking and bill-paying beckon, which could reduce paperwork, but for the foreseeable future, offices need to provide plenty of space for paper filing and flexible computer arrangements to allow for expanding electronic requirements.

As well as computers, our offices need to accommodate printers, scanners, possibly palm pilots, hubs, telephones, and fax machines. If you hope to stow away some of these machines in cupboards, this needs to be factored in at the planning stage to ensure they are built to the right proportions.

◀ Fitting design

One of the banes of modern offices is the spider's web of computer cables, and here is an ideal solution. A desktop running along two walls provides plenty of workspace and gives ample opportunity to hide the dreaded wires. Drawers and shelves under the left-hand desktop provide ample accommodation for files and stationery.

◀◀ Secret order

The key to an orderly office is plenty of filing space for sorting everything away. This floor-to-ceiling cupboard is ideal, as it can be stacked with meticulously labeled boxes.

◀◀◀ Simple solutions

Laptop computers offer the most versatile office solution. They can be taken to any table in the house, while files and other messy office paraphernalia can be stored neatly in a closet elsewhere.

TAKE ONE ROOM:
Streamlined Office

Modern offices have to accommodate ever increasing amounts of technology, especially if one member of the family works from home and school-age children need Internet and computer access for homework. All this takes up both office and desk space, and spawns yards of unsightly cable—certainly until cordless computer links become the norm.

Although this office has only the one computer, it neatly addresses the cable and other office machine issues with an under-desk cabinet. It also provides plenty of strong shelving; still a necessity while paper records are required. Office décor needs to be calming to encourage efficient working. Clean and simple in white and steel, with only wooden office chairs for contrast, this one perfectly fits the bill.

Office décor needs to be simple and calming to encourage efficient and organized working.

REFERENCE POINT

■ Flooring in the home office should be practical and enduring. Wood laminates and linoleum are two good options. See pages 82–85 for guidance.

■ Lighting, too, is an important issue. See pages 146–153.

■ The shade in this office is a roller; for other ideas see pages 132–135.

238

All-cream files provide visual continuity and a sense of order and calm.

A complete wall of box shelving allows for plenty of filing space. Paperwork, magazines, and books are very heavy, so the shelves must have plenty of support. Here they have been given vertical struts for extra strength.

White shades match the walls, keeping the overall color scheme clean and restful.

A desk lamp supplements the general lighting. This is necessary for evening paperwork. Make sure it does not light the computer, however, as it would create glare on the screen.

A high-backed office chair is ergonomically designed for comfortable desk working. It supports the back, and is adjustable so your hands can be at exactly the right height for the keyboard. This is an important factor in avoiding repetitive strain injuries.

The under-desk cabinet houses a printer, keeping the desktop clear for paperwork. It also hides the cables necessary for a modern electronic office.

A roomy waste basket is essential for efficient working, allowing the worker to clear paper even before it hits the desk. Stainless steel works well with white and gray.

A linoleum floor is resilient, easy to keep clean, and withstands potential ink stains caused by dropped pens. The pale gray complements the white interior.

Sunrooms & Porches

Relax and unwind in those special parts of the home where the interior meets the great outdoors.

▲ Cool customer

When the sun gets too hot for enjoyable garden living, retire to the porch, where you can enjoy the fresh air far more comfortably, safely ensconced in the cool shade.

◀ Summerhouse living

Sheltered from the wind, sunrooms extend the outdoor living season. In this home, you could be forgiven for thinking it was summer all year round as it is furnished with garden tables and chairs, a pure white cloth, and plenty of fresh and potted flowers.

◀◀ Informal dining

The long, narrow nature of this porch is ideally suited to alfresco dining. There's nothing expecially exotic about this simple garden table, but painted white and paired with white mesh chairs, the whole scene is restrained by day and magical at twilight.

Relaxed Living

The appeal of garden rooms, verandas, and porches lies in their informality. Furnishings have a garden feel, sometimes taking flowers and plants as their inspiration, sometimes just veering towards simplicity with easy checks or stripes. They are also invariably light and sunny, allowing us to soak up even those watery-sunshine winter days.

Keep it cool: However, especially in conservatories, which have glass roofs, that very sunshine can cause problems. Acting as a greenhouse, the room can get way too hot, plants can wilt, and fabrics can quickly fade. The solution is to install special conservatory shades, which are usually custom-made for individual panes of glass and can be operated individually, so the glare can be cut out while letting in light.

▶ Garden delight

This garden room has all the feel of a summerhouse: a wonderful sunny aspect that just invites you to relax and unwind amid unpretentious cotton furnishings. Stripes always look fresh and have that relaxed feel that is a prerequisite of life in a garden room. They also go very well with other neutral-toned fabrics.

▼ Floral tribute

Lightweight wicker furniture with decoratively covered floral cushions are a favorite conservatory furnishing style. Roses straight from the garden complement the upholstery while simultaneously exuding a gloriously fresh perfume. The outdoor feel is complemented by copious lush, oversized indoor plants.

TAKE ONE ROOM:

Outdoor Living

This porch, with windows on all sides, is all but outdoors. With plenty of room for both sitting and dining, you could live here almost all summer, cooled during the hottest of days by the ceiling fans, and insect-protected in the evenings by mosquito netting and citronella candles. The soft, celadon-green woodwork is easy to live with and complements the greens of the garden. Teamed with the bleached cedar decking, the basic design harmonizes incredibly well with the outdoor surrounding.

For relaxed living, design porches that are easy to maintain. Cedar decking can be quickly washed down with a brush and water at the end of the day, leaving it scrubbed clear of garden debris, ship-shape style. Deep-toned upholstery means minor marks do not become an issue, and a dark-topped table needs no cloth—which could either stain or blow off in the breeze.

For relaxed living, design porches that are easy to maintain.

REFERENCE POINT

■ If you want to style your porch so that you further emphasize the indoor atmosphere, a perfect accessory is a rug. Easy to carry and easy to sweep, your choice is wide. See pages 88–89.

■ A sofa in your sunroom or on your porch adds a real sense of luxury. Before buying one, however, read the advice on pages 140–143.

Celadon green is an ideal color for any garden room. Here, it has been used on all the wood surfaces to echo the natural surroundings.

Ceiling fans take the heat out of the hottest days. Their lazy rhythm contributes to a peaceful ambience.

A candle housed in a hurricane lamp can be lit as the sun goes down for a romantic atmosphere. Use citronella candles if you want to deter biting insects.

Glass-free windows are protected in inclement weather with pull-down shutters. Insect screens prevent mosquitoes from spoiling the peace and quiet.

245

There's no comfort sacrificed on this porch—the sofas and chairs are fully upholstered for all-day luxury. The rich plum tones of the sofa seats accentuate the predominantly cream and green décor.

A simple trestle table and rush-seated chairs add to the outdoorsy feel—a perfect, unpretentious style for serving simple and fresh salad lunches. The black tabletop adds definition to the whole scheme without compromising on the informal surroundings.

Photography Credits

The publisher would like to thank the following photographers for supplying the pictures in this book:

Page 1 Dana Gallagher; **2** Peter Aaron/Esto; **3** Tim Street-Porter; **4** Jonn Coolidge; **5 top** Courtesy of *House Beautiful*; **5 bottom** Jonn Coolidge; **6** Tim Street-Porter; **8–9** Nigel Young; **10 bottom** Bill Holt; **10 top** Luca Trovato; **11** Jonn Coolidge; **12** Laura Resen; **13 left** Courtesy of *House Beautiful*; **13 right** Jonn Coolidge; **14** Jonn Coolidge; **15** Scott Frances; **16** Courtesy of *House Beautiful*; **17** Scott Frances; **18 left** Laura Resen; **18 right** Jonn Coolidge; **19** Mick Hales; **20** Jonn Coolidge; **21 left** Fernando Bengoechea; **21 right** Jonn Coolidge; **22 left** Courtesy of *House Beautiful*; **22 right** Tim Beddow; **23** Timothy Hursley; **24** Tim Street-Porter; **25** Gordon Beall; **26** Nigel Young; **27** Laura Resen; **28** C. Gardenti; **29 left** Laura Resen; **29 right** Dominique Vorillon; **30–31** William Waldron; **32 left** Scott Frances; **32 right** Jeff McNamara; **33** Tim Beddow; **34** Peter Margonelli; **35** Courtesy of *House Beautiful*; **36 left** Peter Margonelli; **36 right** Jonn Coolidge; **37** Peter Margonelli; **38** Randy Foulds; **39** Susan Gentry McWhinney; **40 left** David Prince; **40 right** Steven Randazzo; **41** Steven Randazzo; **42 left** Jonn Coolidge; **42 right** Tim Street-Porter; **43** Fernando Bengoechea; **45** Courtesy of *House Beautiful*; **46 bottom** Scott Frances; **46 top** Thibault Jeanson; **47** Jonn Coolidge; **49** Pieter Estersohn; **50 left** Anthony Cotsifas; **50 right** Dana Gallagher; **51** Christopher Petkanas; **53** Scott Frances; **54 left** Anita Calero; **54 right** William Waldron; **55** Simon Upton; **57** Gordon Beall; **58 left** Toshi Otsuki; **58 right** Antoine Bootz; **59** Jeremy Samuelson; **61** Jeff McNamara; **62 left** Jonn Coolidge; **62 right** Courtesy of *House Beautiful*; **63** Robert Lautman; **65** Peter Aaron/Esto; **66** William Waldron; **67** William Waldron; **69** William Waldron; **70 left** Simon Upton; **70 right** Courtesy of *House Beautiful*; **71** Eric Boman; **73** Jan Tham; **74–75** Nigel Young; **76 left** Dana Gallagher; **76 top right** William Waldron; **76 bottom right** Thibault Jeanson; **77** Courtesy of *House Beautiful*; **78** Jonn Coolidge; **79** Tria Giovan; **80** Fernando Bengoechea; **81** Tim Beddow; **82** William P. Steele; **83** Jonn Coolidge; **84** Luca Trovato; **85** Victoria Pearson; **86** Dana Gallagher; **87** Frank Heckers; **88** Andreas von Einsiedel; **89** Jonn Coolidge; **90** Jeff McNamara; **91** Jeff McNamara; **92** Courtesy of *House Beautiful*; **93 left** Dana Gallagher; **93 right** Christopher Petkanas; **94 left** Minh + Wass; **94 right** Elizabeth Zeschin; **95** William Waldron; **96** Dana Gallagher; **97** Fernando Bengoechea; **98** Jonn Coolidge; **99 left** Mick Hales; **99 right** Tria Giovan; **100 left** Tim Street-Porter; **100 right** Tria Giovan; **101 top** Courtesy of *House Beautiful*; **101 bottom** Courtesy of *House Beautiful*; **102 top** Simon Upton; **102 bottom** William Waldron; **103** Dana Gallagher; **104 top** Nigel Young; **104 bottom** Peter Margonelli; **105** Anthony Cotsifas; **108** William Waldron; **111** Jonn Coolidge; **112** Fernando Bengoechea; **114** William P. Steele **116** Oberto Gili; **117** Courtesy of *House Beautiful*; **118** Jonn Coolidge; **120** Tim Street-Porter; **121** Antoine Bootz; **122 left** Dominique Vorillon; **122 right** David Montgomery; **123** Dominique Vorillon; **124 left** William Waldron; **124 right** Toshi Otsuki; **125** Fernando Bengoechea; **126 left** Fernando Bengoechea; **126 right** Toshi Otsuki; **128 left** Steven Randazzo; **128 right** Tim Beddow; **129** Toshi Otsuki; **130** Paul Whicheloe; **131** Gross & Daley; **132 top** Peter Margonelli; **132 bottom** Dominique Vorillon; **133** Toshi Otsuki; **134** Courtesy of *House Beautiful*; **135** David Glomb; **136** Jeff McNamara; **138 left** Jeff McNamara; **138 right** Paul Whicheloe; **139** Tim Street-Porter; **140** Jonn Coolidge; **141** Courtesy of *House Beautiful*; **142 left** Courtesy of *House Beautiful*; **143 right** Jeff McNamara; **144** Jonn Coolidge; **144** Simon Watson; **145** Simon Watson; **146 left** Jonn Coolidge; **146 right** Katherine Bogert; **147** Paul Whicheloe; **148** Peter Margonelli; **150 left** Thibault Jeanson; **150 right** Jonn Coolidge; **152** Courtesy of *House Beautiful*; **154 left** Jean-François Jaussaud; **154 right** Fernando Bengoechea; **155** Bob Hiemstra; **156 top** Paul Whicheloe; **156 bottom** Dominique Vorillon; **157** Scott Frances; **158** Scott Frances; **159** Courtesy of *House Beautiful*; **160–161** Scott Frances; **162 left top** William Waldron; **162 left bottom** Mick Hales; **162 right** Evan Sklar; **163** Tim Street-Porter; **164 left** Courtesy of *House Beautiful*; **164 right** Jonn Coolidge; **165** Timothy Hursley; **166** Andreas von Einsiedel; **168 left** William Waldron; **168 right** Bob Hiemstra; **169** Scott Frances; **170** Courtesy of *House Beautiful*; **172 left** Tim Street-Porter; **172 right** Fritz von der Schulenburg; **173** Courtesy of *House Beautiful*; **174** Toshi Otsuki; **175** Christopher Simon Sykes; **176** William Waldron; **177 top** Fernando Bengoechea; **177 bottom** Courtesy of *House Beautiful*; **178** Scott Frances; **179** Peter Margonelli; **180** Jonn Coolidge; **182 left** Tria Giovan; **182 right** Courtesy of *House Beautiful*; **183** Lisa Romerein; **184** Jonathan Wallen; **185** Oberto Gili; **186** Tim Street-Porter; **187** Jonn Coolidge; **188 left** Courtesy of *House Beautiful*; **188 right** Bill Holt; **189** Alec Hemer; **190 left** Richard Barnes; **190 right** Tria Giovan; **191** Simon Upton; **192** William Waldron; **193 top** Jeff McNamara; **193 bottom** Jeff McNamara; **194** Scott Frances; **196** Courtesy of *House Beautiful*; **197 top left** Courtesy of *House Beautiful*; **197 top right** William Waldron; **197 bottom** Bill Holt; **198** Eric Boman; **199** Edmund Barr; **200** Jonn Coolidge; **201** Fernando Bengoechea; **202** Tim Street-Porter; **204** Steven Randazzo; **205 left** Toshi Otsuki; **205 right** Steven Randazzo; **206 top** William Waldron; **206 bottom** Scott Frances; **207 left** William Waldron; **207 right** Courtesy of *House Beautiful*; **208** Jeremy Samuelson; **209 top** Toshi Otsuki; **209 bottom** Courtesy of *House Beautiful*; **210 left** Tom McWilliam; **210 right** Courtesy of *House Beautiful*; **211 top left** Dana Gallagher; **211 top right** Jonn Coolidge; **211 bottom** Courtesy of *House Beautiful*; **212 left** Tim Beddow; **212 right** Tim Street-Porter; **213** Courtesy of *House Beautiful*; **214** Laura Resen; **215 left** Toshi Otsuki; **215 right** Toshi Otsuki; **216** Michael Mundy; **218 left top** Lisa Romerein; **218 left bottom** Courtesy of *House Beautiful*; **218 right** Scott Frances; **219** Grazia Branco; **220 left** Courtesy of *House Beautiful*; **220 right** Jonn Coolidge; **221** Jim Cooper; **222** Courtesy of *House Beautiful*; **223** Courtesy of *House Beautiful*; **224 left** Luke White; **224 right** Gordon Beall; **225** Toshi Otsuki; **226** William Waldron; **228 left** Elizabeth Zeschin; **228 right** David Phelps; **229** Anita Calero; **230 top** Susan Gentry McWhinney; **230 bottom** Susan Gentry McWhinney; **231** Susan Gentry McWhinney; **232** Dana Gallagher; **234 left** Courtesy of *House Beautiful*; **234 right** Jon Jensen; **235** Ila Duncan; **236 left** Jon Jensen; **236 right** Jacques Dirand; **237** Jonn Coolidge; **238** Jonn Coolidge; **240 left** Courtesy of *House Beautiful*; **240 right** Eric Boman; **241** William Waldron; **242** Eric Boman; **243** Roger Davies; **244** Eric Boman; **246** Timothy Hursley.

Index